Dev(... l
an

A ses ... ch

Routledge

This third edition published 2012
by Routledge
2 Park Square, Milton Park, Abingdon, Oxon OX14 4RN

Simultaneously published in the USA and Canada
by Routledge
711 Third Avenue, New York, NY 10017

Routledge is an imprint of the Taylor & Francis Group, an informa business

© 2012 Maggie Carroll and Jackie Hannay

British Library Cataloguing in Publication Data
A catalogue record for this book is available from the British Library

Library of Congress Cataloging-in-Publication Data
Carroll, M. E.
  Developing physical health, fitness and well-being through
  gymnastics (7–11): a session-by-session approach/Maggie Carroll,
  Jackie Hannay. – 2nd ed.
  p. cm.
  1. Gymnastics for children.   2. Movement education.
  I. Hannay, Jackie.   II. Title.
  GV464.5.C35 2011
  796.44083′41 – dc22   2010051765

ISBN: 978–0–415–59109–6 (hbk)
ISBN: 978–0–415–59108–9 (pbk)
ISBN: 978–0–203–81342–3 (ebk)

Typeset in Bembo
by Florence Production Ltd, Stoodleigh, Devon

Printed and bound in India by Replika Press Pvt. Ltd.

Contents

Preface

We were delighted to be asked to write new editions of my original teachers' gymnastics workbooks for primary school teachers and students.

(The first series was co-authored by Bob Garner and Maggie, and the second by Hazel Manners and Maggie.)

The need for this new edition became self-evident for two reasons:

● The success of the series and its format, as evidenced by ongoing testimonies from teachers and students on its usefulness and clarity.

● Inevitable changes to the primary curriculum over time have necessitated our re-evaluation of the principles underlying the teaching of gymnastic activity. Many of these still pertain but, additionally, we have focused more of the work on children's well-being, and on how it also supports access to broad learning across the curriculum.

We have retained a similar format and approach as in the original versions because teachers have told us how this has made their planning and assessment straightforward and manageable.

We welcome this opportunity to share with teachers and students this contribution to a crucial aspect of children's development.

Maggie Carroll
Jackie Hannay
University of Brighton, January 2011

Acknowledgements

Photographs: Les Cross, Principal Technician, University of Brighton
Illustrations: Marilyn Amos
Children: Grovelands County Primary School, Hastings

Foreword

The updating of this book is very welcome. It has always been a most valuable resource for the primary school subject leader, experienced teacher and, especially, the non-specialist. The lesson outlines have a clear structure with a good range of activities that, when sequenced, help learners to develop specific sets of skills and apply them appropriately. The units are well designed with development of core skills, specific techniques and compositional concepts and ideas central to them. In addition, there is a very clear section in each lesson that helps teachers to know what to look for in terms of specific learning objectives. It also makes excellent use of the core tasks developed as part of Curriculum 2000 and, subsequently, the PESSYP strategy.

Carroll and Hannay have skilfully updated the materials in order to reflect both the most recent curriculum developments in physical education and the most up-to-date thinking about teaching and learning. Whatever happens to the National Curriculum, the book will provide a really strong starting point for the development of positive learning experiences in this area of physical education. For subject leaders, the authors provide an excellent resource to support the development of schemes of work and a 'feel safe' clear set of ideas that can be turned into lesson plans for the non-specialist. For those who use the resource well, it will enable high-quality curriculum, learning experiences and teaching to be provided for all learners. This will offer settings in which children, whatever their ability, can develop:

- physical competency;
- confidence in themselves as physical beings;
- creativity and performance skills; and
- knowledge and understanding of aspects of personal health and well-being and healthy lifestyles.

Crichton Casbon
Crichton Casbon Consulting Ltd.
www.cccreates.co.uk

Introduction

Physical skills develop from the moment children are born. It is during the early years of children's lives (3–7) that physical education (PE) is primarily concerned with all-round physical development, and young children need to be provided with opportunities to explore a range of physical movement and equipment through structured and exploratory play in order to develop and master key motor skills. (See the companion volume, *Developing Physical Health and Well-being through Gymnastic Activity (5–7)*.)

However, in the later primary years (7–11), children are becoming capable of differentiated activity, which is more closely aligned to those forms of activity seen in the public domain. They are able to develop and perform carefully controlled movements and sequences that are pleasing both to watch and perform, and that need skill in their execution.

Development of this will occur only through regular activity during the middle and later primary school phases. Whatever form a national curriculum might take in the primary years of schooling, concern for physical development, health and well-being must predominate, and as such is vital for children's development as confident individuals. It provides the foundations for long-term well-being and contributes to children's all-round development.

This workbook sets out to ensure that gymnastics, as part of a balanced PE programme, offers opportunities for children to acquire aspects of:

- physical skill acquisition and performance, which are improved through practice (they will become competent in the control and dexterity of their movements, and will use these abilities creatively and with commitment);

- generic skills so that they can move in controlled ways in a range of different contexts; and

- broader learning across the curriculum, often related to their personal, emotional and social development.

Building on work from the early years, where the children will have begun to master natural actions of rolling, climbing, running, jumping and sliding, combined with controlling the weight of the body while moving, the focus is now different. Children will need to concentrate more particularly on 'correctness', on control and on the beauty of their movements. They will continue to learn longer or more complex sequences that they are able to replicate and develop towards an optimum performance. They will continue to cooperate effectively with others in this, observing, giving and asking for feedback, and striving towards the notion of 'getting it right'.

Gynmastics sessions will provide the ideal context for later primary-aged children to refine their social skills, such as communicating, negotiating, taking the lead and sharing ideas. They will also be able to challenge themselves by developing a deepening knowledge of what is good work. All this needs to be planned for and its development supported. For example, to be able to give feedback to another is a sophisticated skill that will have been introduced in the early primary years, and now needs to be developed to ensure that it is accurate, is given in a positive manner and benefits the receiver.

Through the mastery of skills and through achievement, children will be able to develop their sense of worth and well-being. This, combined with their developing knowledge and understanding of such matters as nutrition, hygiene and sleep, and the importance of achieving a balance of these, will allow them to make informed choices and engage in a healthy lifestyle. Children's engagement in gymnastics will, in part, provide a framework for them to gain this knowledge and expertise.

Links can be made to other areas of the curriculum in order to enhance children's learning, but these should not be contrived. Indeed, other areas of PE may lend themselves more appropriately to cross-curricular work, especially in the outside learning environment.

Gymnastics develops children's strength, balance, speed, suppleness, stamina and core body skills, as well as posture. These have importance for other areas of the PE programme. For example, to be successful games players, children need to have many of these attributes.

The use of information and communications technology (ICT) has a key part to play in teaching gymnastic activity. In the later section, 'So what about assessment?' (page 7), ICT is considered to be an essential assessment tool that can be used with the children to enable the teacher to capture performances. Together with the teacher, the children will be able to evaluate and celebrate their achievements.

What is involved in gymnastics?

Definitions are often difficult and imprecise. A definition of gymnastics is not necessarily helpful – yet it is necessary to know what characterises the work. It would seem that, whatever form of gymnastics is evident (Olympic, rhythmic, educational, sports, acrobatics, vaulting and agility), certain kinds of attributes give the work its name.

Gymnastics is normally characterised as having components such as:

- physical (strength and suppleness/flexibility);
- skill (with or without apparatus);
- aesthetic (shape, line and finish);
- creative (choosing movements that are authentically gymnastic);
- cognitive (understanding what the body is doing); and
- psychological (perseverance, courage and determination).

This list, however, need not deter teachers. They do not need to be gymnasts themselves, nor have detailed knowledge of complex gymnastics skills. Throughout Key Stage 1, children will have been developing their physical and motor skills, exploring basic movements, such as jumps, balance, travelling, rolls etc., and developing their knowledge of their own physical development, their health and their well-being. In doing this, the characteristic components of gymnastics will gradually have emerged through these early years. So now, in Key Stage 2, as noted above, the emphasis is on the need for children to concentrate more particularly on 'correctness', on control and on the beauty of their movements, learning longer or more complex sequences leading towards optimum performance.

If the six components of gymnastics listed above need to be present for the activity to be authentic, and if the work is to happen in school, then a teaching approach throughout must be adopted that, on the one hand, will generate the development of these essential characteristics and, on the other, will also be a relevant educational experience. Children should therefore be able to demonstrate bodily skill on the floor, on apparatus, on their own and with a partner, and in a small group, with the ultimate aim of creating a performance.

How do teachers achieve this aim?

As in the early years, the individual needs of the children must be considered. The early years child will have been using 'gymnastic' activities to explore a range of movements and the role of the teacher at this stage was to intervene to make the children *conscious* of what they were doing (so that they were both *moving* and *knowing*). Further to this, the teacher will also have been developing the children's knowledge of the criteria that they need to consider in order to improve and achieve the desired outcome.

Now, however, as the children develop through the middle and later phases in the primary school years, the teacher seeks to develop more stylised, skilled bodily actions – which have a clearer resemblance to recognised gymnastics forms. By the end of Key Stage 2, children should be capable of demonstrating a range of skilled, controlled and refined body actions that they have combined in a sequence, achieved through a selection and combination of movements (with consideration of levels, speed and direction), assessment and refinement. Through this cycle children will work towards achieving their ultimate performance.

If gymnastics is about bodily skill (as it undoubtedly is), and if we want our children to be proficient in using skilled bodily movement in answer to various kinds of tasks, the style of teaching must operate fully along the methodological continuum of open-ended (process) to closed (product). It makes sense that some activities require direct teaching (some skills for example), whereas others lend themselves to an experimental approach. Sometimes the teacher will set tasks that tightly constrain what the children may do (for example, 'spring from feet to hands to feet' or 'practise performing cartwheels'). At other times, children may need to demonstrate understanding of a movement concept in their performance and so the task will be of a different order (for example, 'change from one action to another using rotation to start/initiate the changes'). There are also many other stages in between that are more or less constraining. Examples of all these kinds of task feature in the session plans that follow.

Ultimately, for children to succeed they need to enjoy gymnastics. This can only be achieved by ensuring that they all experience success, and therefore teachers need to cater for individual needs. Children usually respond positively to challenges, and so these need to be built into the sessions to ensure that they are achievable and celebrated. Opportunities to share successes may be extended outside the class through performing to other classes, in assemblies, to parents and within the community.

Creating a positive ethos in sessions will optimise children's learning. If children feel that their abilities are recognised, that their ideas have been valued and that they have felt safe, they are more likely to experience a smooth transition to the next Key Stage of their schooling. Gymnastics sessions are well suited to promoting such an ethos.

The place of skill in the later years

It is evident that young children are flexible, agile and inquisitive. Through gymnastic activity we want to channel these traits in the older primary-aged children so that they become skilful in managing their bodies in a variety of situations. In Key Stage 1, the emphasis was on skilful control of the actions the child has chosen rather than mastery of gymnastic skills chosen by the teacher. The focus was on the individual children's needs within the class, where there is inevitably a wide ability range. To some extent this will be the case in Key Stage 2, as it is likely that one child has a relatively immature stage of development whereas another is able to control and use bodily skill responsively. So, whereas most children will be ready to focus on the work that is more characteristically 'gymnastic', a few may still need the emphasis more aligned to Key Stage 1 work. In order to extend the children's capability, the 'Specific skills guide' (page 215) sets out a clear and safe process for teaching gymnastics skills. Throughout the four-year overall plan, in particular sessions and where skill teaching is appropriate, teachers are asked to refer to this guide.

When a set skill is to be taught (for example, see Year 4, sessions 12 and 13), it is suggested that the teacher asks an able child to demonstrate exactly the skill task being set. The class observes. Then, in order for the teacher to give further support to the skill practice, the class, in groups, works on differentiated tasks, leaving the teacher to remain with the group practising the skill.

In their classes, teachers may have several children who have been taught gymnastic skills at a club. These children may be very skilful in this respect and teachers may be apprehensive about safety factors, or worry that other children may emulate them. This is why, on the whole, most of the content of the sessions in this workbook calls for individual, inventive responses quite different from the way gymnastics clubs operate. However, the more able children can often be a source of inspiration for others, and especially will be able to share ideas and demonstrate good quality.

Teachers may have to explain this to the children who want just to perform their skills, and, additionally, encourage them to be inventive by trying other ways of answering the tasks set. If teachers use the ideas outlined in the sessions, they will be able to broaden children's movement vocabulary and develop their performance capabilities.

So what about assessment?

Assessment for learning and of learning should be integral to the gymnastics session. Teachers will need to assess the children's physical competence and also the extent to which there is increasing development of their understanding of health, well-being and cross-curricular aspects of learning (concern for others, safety, giving and receiving feedback etc.).

In addition to teacher assessment, the children should be encouraged to engage in self-assessment and peer-assessment. Examples of these will be found in the session plans that follow.

In the sessions, children will be trying out movements, reflecting on them and then refining them. So they will need to learn about the kinds of criteria against which they will be able to assess themselves and others, and, in so doing, begin to take responsibility for their own development and learning. The teacher can use different strategies to achieve this:

- modelling and demonstration of good practice;
- mini-plenary sessions to reinforce expectations; and
- reviewing performances with focused feedback.

Children should be encouraged to discuss and evaluate their work at the end of each session in preparation for the next. These opportunities can happen in the classroom after the lesson.

Judiciously planned use of ICT will also help the children and the teachers in this process as they record, observe and assess themselves in action.

The approach

In order to facilitate teachers' selection of session content and its presentation to the children, the workbook is written in a session-by-session format (called the 'session plan' and starting on page 75) for the four years of Key Stage 2. The sessions can be adapted, developed or used for consolidation, dependent on the time and resources available and/or the children's ability levels. Most sessions indicate the work to be covered over a two-week period, but teachers should spend more time if needed to ensure the work is of a high quality. They should not be afraid of repeating sessions to achieve this. This is important. Teachers must be confident in spending enough time to enable the children to 'play' with ideas, to practise and then to 'get it right'.

The individual sessions are preceded by an 'overall plan' (starting on page 17), which will give teachers an overview of the programme to be taught over each of the four years.

The overall plan

The plan sets out the focus, aspects for consolidation and the learning objectives for all the sessions in Years 3–6, and in this way shows the progression that has been built into the whole four-year programme.

This plan is a continuation of the work from Key Stage 1, and so will support the transition process and avoid regression in the children's learning. (See the companion volume, *Developing Physical Health and Well-being through Gymnastic Activity (5–7)*.) It also indicates how the Year 6 work may lead into that found in Year 7.

The session plan

The session plan is a detailed plan derived from the overall plan. It is an easy-to-follow guide for teachers and student teachers in delivering the sessions. Each year has eleven session plans, nine of these incorporating at least two week's work, but with a single assessment session at the start and end of each year. Each plan has:

- *a title* that forms the focus for the session;
- *learning objectives* relating to physical development, to aspects of general health and well-being and to aspects of broader learning across the curriculum;
- *assessment criteria* that indicate the questions the teachers and the children should be asking themselves about what has been learned.

In most cases consolidation from the previous session is built into the plan.

All sessions have warm-up, floor work and final activities. Most have apparatus too. After each session, it is suggested that the children spend a few minutes recording what they have performed in some form of a workbook, and also discuss what they thought they had done well and what they need to do to improve their performance. It is particularly important to use this time to help the children articulate their understanding of their performances and how to improve upon them, particularly as the length and complexity of their sequences increase as they move from Year 3 to Year 6.

Additionally, teachers might wish to discuss issues of health and well-being just after the sessions. They might also do this after the session warm-up, where there is often a focus on developing suppleness and strength.

Warm-up

This should be vigorous so that the children have the opportunity to develop strength, speed, flexibility and stamina.

At the start of each session, there are tasks designed to get the body warm, raise the heart rate, and so prepare the body for the stretching (and sometimes strengthening) activities that follow.

Warm-ups can provide additional opportunities for children to consolidate skills and actions learned in previous sessions. They also enable teachers to incorporate activities that support children's learning about their personal well-being, as they are actively experiencing changes in how they are feeling, for example breathing heavily when active.

As noted above, in most sessions there is a specific emphasis on developing suppleness and strength.

Floor work

This centres on the development of skills and actions. It provides opportunities to select and refine these skills and combine them in a sequence, working towards an ultimate performance. Within the sessions, through demonstration, observation, modelling, questioning and reflection, children will gain an understanding of the performance criteria that will encourage them to take responsibility for their own learning and so become independent learners. Through this they will have opportunities to develop skills such as problem solving, sharing ideas and giving feedback. There is an increasing emphasis on partner work and then group work as the sessions move through the years. This facilitates children's development in cooperative learning in this unique context.

Apparatus work

This is used as an extension of the floor work. During Key Stage 1 children will have learned to lift, carry and assemble apparatus appropriately, placing it in arrangements devised by the teacher and then by themselves (see the section 'Apparatus diagrams' on page 229).

Children should be encouraged to continue to replicate ideas and skills developed on the floor and explore these on the apparatus. They will discover that they may have to adapt their movements on the apparatus. The teacher should encourage them to be constantly active, in order to maximise the opportunity for the development of stamina, strength, speed and flexibility.

As the children become more adept and skilful, they will spend more time refining their performances. As in floor work, there is a developing emphasis on working with a partner and in small groups throughout the programme.

Final activity

Often this includes a strengthening exercise, and is also an opportunity for the children to feel and understand the benefits of effective stretching after activity.

The content of the sessions varies so that there are:

- activities done together (including the teacher) to develop a corporate sense of belonging;
- challenges in which children, through exploration, try to find their own way of responding, working individually and with others, discovering their capabilities;
- ideas from the teacher and from the children, put forward to help the children create patterns of movements that can be repeated and performed. This will support their sequencing skills and their movement memories.

As noted earlier, it is very important that teachers give the children sufficient time to try out ideas, practise them and then work towards the best quality of which they are capable.

Differentiation

Within the sessions, the teacher will need to ensure all the children have opportunities to engage and achieve. This is essential for individual progression, and is likely to take place at different rates. To support differentiation the teacher will consider, for example, how much input is given, the length of sequences and whether the children work individually or in pairs, or sometimes in larger groups.

The following are suggested ways of enabling children to extend their work when the teacher sees that they are ready for moving a step further:

- refine the sequences with new 'starting' and finishing' positions;
- combine movements to show clear changes in direction, speed (where appropriate) or levels;
- add an additional action to the sequence;
- add a named skill to the sequence;
- consider using short phrases of music to accompany the performances.

Children should be continuously working on the quality of their movement – for example:

- extension in the feet and toes, the arms and hands, and the head, in line with the movement;
- strong body tension.

The assessment activities and assessment criteria

The use of assessment activities in sessions 1 and 20 in all four years will allow teachers to find out what the children can do, what they know and what they understand. They will then have knowledge of the individual so that they can build upon, extend and measure progress. The teachers can then use this information, as appropriate, as a reference point for the next session(s) they teach. As it is difficult for teachers to monitor all the class, it is important that varied resources are used, where appropriate, to support this process. For example, ICT in the form of the digital camera and the camcorder are ideal to record children's movements. Teaching assistants may also be asked to offer support in this respect.

Teachers may wish to consider the benefits of involving those children who are unable to participate in a session, in taking a focused evaluative role or even recording the work.

Children can learn to observe others' movements and this will help their understanding, assist their language development and increase the range of activities they can do. This form of assessment (peer-assessment) is an integral part of all the sessions that follow.

All sessions should include opportunities for children to show their work (performance) individually, in pairs, in small groups or to the whole class (which could be in mini-plenary periods in the middle and at the end of sessions, giving opportunities for ongoing feedback).

The place of demonstration and modelling

Built into the session plans are opportunities for children to see others' work, in order to promote understanding of worthwhile performance. Demonstrations by individual children need to be purposeful. Half the class watching the rest can prove to be a non-productive use of precious time, unless those observing are asked to look at an identified small group of children.

The teacher can select a child to show the rest in the event of a specific task about to be attempted, for example the placement of the hands when practising a cartwheel. Or a child may be selected to show others how he/she has responded to a task, demonstrating inventiveness/creativity, so that other children can try this for themselves. Others may be chosen to show particularly good quality work – they will be modelling the quality to which the others may aspire, for example the powerful thrust needed in the take-off for an effective leap.

In all instances it is best to confirm with the child first that he/she is prepared to demonstrate, and all demonstrations should be followed up by discussion with the children about what they have seen.

In certain circumstances, where the teacher has confidence, he/she may demonstrate a movement for the children to inform the improvement of their performance, or the accuracy of what they are trying to do.

There are examples of all these ideas in the sessions in Years 3–6.

The place of music

In the latter sessions of Year 6, there are opportunities for the children to use music to accompany their work. This often generates some most interesting sequences. The music chosen should be relatively simple, with clear phrases, and should be quite short. We have suggested that the children might wish to bring in their own music too.

Apparatus

This workbook ideally requires the following apparatus for a class of thirty children to ensure maximum activity:

- 6 benches
- 10 mats
- 4 planks
- 3 stools/stacking tables
- 1 bar box
- 1 springboard (Reuther model, if possible)
- 1 climbing frame (with ropes)
- 2 agility/movement tables.

Organisation

It is the responsibility of the teacher to make sure that any children handling apparatus do so correctly and safely.

In the section 'Apparatus diagrams and task cards' (page 229), we have included suggestions for the layout of apparatus when specific tasks are set (see Year 5, sessions 10 and 11). Otherwise we believe the children are capable of deciding where to place the pieces they have chosen, under the guidance of the teacher. Apparatus MUST always be checked by the teacher before use.

The children should put out the apparatus in such a way that there is still space to explore movement on the floor around the apparatus. They should already have learned to lift, carry and place apparatus safely, and to work as a team assembling and dismantling apparatus. They should know where they are placing equipment, and initially this can be helped by sitting the children in the area where the apparatus is to be placed.

Apparatus should be of a suitable height for the children and this should be progressive as the children move through the four years. They should not jump down from a height higher than themselves and mats should be placed where children will be jumping from a piece of apparatus. If children are practising and performing forward and backward rolls, there should always be a mat in place.

The apparatus should be stored at strategic positions around the sides of the room in readiness, so that all children have to do is lift it into position.

Handling the apparatus

As noted above, by Key Stage 2 the children should be proficient in moving apparatus. The following should be noted:

- There should be four children to each heavy piece of equipment – two on each side. They should lift it together and put it down together.

- There should be four children to each mat – two on each side. Holding the mats on the corners should be avoided as this can cause damage. Mats should be lifted and not dragged, and put away tidily.

- Children should always carry equipment walking and, wherever possible, facing forwards.
- All hooks, Velcro® and bolts must be securely in position and the teacher MUST check the apparatus assembly before children use it.

Safety

The safety of the children must be uppermost in the teacher's mind at all times and in accordance with local authority regulations. The Association for Physical Education (afPE) should also be a source of reference (*Safe Practice in Physical Education and School Sport*, 2008).

A general, agreed policy throughout the school will ensure safe and simple guidelines for every teacher.

Note: teachers should take inhalers (for children who require them) and first-aid kits to every session.

The hall

This area in most Key Stage 2 settings is a multi-use space and the following points need to be considered:

- the floor should be clean, splinter-proof and non-slippery;
- the working area needs to be clear of displays, workbook shelves, pianos, overhead projectors, etc., whose corners are dangerous if a child accidentally bumps into them.

Clothing

- Children should change into appropriate clothing for a gymnastics session, such as shorts and a T-shirt.
- Where the floor is suitable the children should work with bare feet.
- Jewellery should not be worn and long hair should be tied back.
- The teacher should also, of course, wear suitable clothing and safe footwear or work with bare feet.

NB: The teacher MUST be positioned where he/she can see the whole class at all times.

Overall plan
Year 3

Session 1

Assessment activity

This first session is for an initial assessment of the children's capabilities to ascertain what they know and what they can do. It has only floor work.

This session relates, in part, to the final assessment tasks in Key Stage 1.

LEARNING OBJECTIVES

(The objectives of the session need to be made explicit to the children. They also need to assess the extent to which they have achieved them.)

Physical

1   To perform three travelling actions in a sequence.
2   To add a starting shape and a rotation action to complete the sequence.
3   To remember and perform the sequence with consistency, coordination and control.

Well-being

4   To articulate the changes happening to the body during activity, and the benefits of being active to health and well-being.

Broader learning

5   To identify actions/movements that they can perform well, and know one or two ways in which to improve.

DISCUSSION

Share ideas about what contributes to staying healthy and well.

Talk about what constitutes good work and how improvements can be made.

ASSESSMENT CRITERIA – QUESTIONS TO CONSIDER

1 Can the children perform three travelling actions in a sequence?

2 Can they add a starting shape and a rotation action to complete their sequence?

3 Can they remember and perform the sequence with consistency, coordination and control?

4 Can the children talk about the changes happening to their bodies when they are active and the benefits of being active to their health and well-being?

5 Can they identify actions/movements that they can perform well, and know one or two ways in which they can improve?

OUTCOME

Some children will achieve, some will excel and some will achieve less.

Sessions 2 and 3

Balance – what is balance?

Consolidation from previous session: to perform three travelling actions in a sequence and perform the sequence with consistency, coordination and control.

LEARNING OBJECTIVES

(The objectives of the session need to be made explicit to the children. They also need to assess the extent to which they have achieved them.)

Physical

1   To know how to balance on different parts of the body using tension and extension.
2   To combine balancing actions by transferring the weight smoothly from one body part to another.

Well-being

3   To know that strength and suppleness are important components of gymnastics.

Broader learning

4   To share ideas with a partner and select actions together to combine in a sequence.

ASSESSMENT CRITERIA – QUESTIONS TO CONSIDER

1   Can the children balance on a variety of body parts with well-held body tension, and with toes and fingers extended?
2   Can children move from taking weight from one body part to another smoothly?
3   Can the children identify physical elements that affect gymnastic performance?
4   Can the children work together to create a sequence using each other's ideas?

Sessions 4 and 5

Balance – what is balance?

Consolidation from previous session: to combine balances on different parts of the body in a sequence on the floor and apparatus.

LEARNING OBJECTIVES

(The objectives of the session need to be made explicit to the children. They also need to assess the extent to which they have achieved them.)

Physical

1   To be able to link balances on small and large body parts.
2   To be able to work with a partner to produce a sequence that can be remembered and performed well.

Well-being

3   To know that muscular strength can be developed through physical activity.

Broader learning

4   To be able to negotiate with a partner to create and adapt a sequence.

ASSESSMENT CRITERIA – QUESTIONS TO CONSIDER

1   Can the children link balances held on small body parts smoothly with balances on large body parts and vice versa?
2   Can they work with a partner and perform a sequence that they have both remembered?
3   Can the children identify that being physically active helps strengthen their muscles and heart?
4   Can children work together with one another to create a sequence using each other's ideas on the floor and apparatus?

Sessions 6 and 7

Balance – related to shape

Consolidation from previous session: to combine balances on small parts of the body with large body part balances.

LEARNING OBJECTIVES

(The objectives of the session need to be made explicit to the children. They also need to assess the extent to which they have achieved them.)

Physical

1 To be able to balance holding different body shapes.
2 To improve performance using particular criteria for evaluation.

Well-being

3 To know some of the benefits to health and well-being of physical activity.

Broader learning

4 To name particular muscle groups.

ASSESSMENT CRITERIA – QUESTIONS TO CONSIDER

1 Can the children perform balances holding stretched, tucked, narrow and wide shapes?
2 Can the children explain what they have to do to improve their movements and then take action?
3 Can children articulate some benefits of engaging in an active lifestyle?
4 Can children name one or two leg muscle groups, for example hamstring, quadriceps, calf?

Sessions 8 and 9

Balance – related to apparatus

Consolidation from previous session: to combine a variety of balances showing a range of body shapes (including tucked, narrow, stretched and wide).

LEARNING OBJECTIVES

(The objectives of the session need to be made explicit to the children. They also need to assess the extent to which they have achieved them.)

Physical

1   To be able to balance on the apparatus in a variety of ways.
2   To know what is meant by distributing weight.

Well-being

3   To be able to identify how the body feels after being active and why this is beneficial.

Broader learning

4   To be able to name particular muscle groups.

ASSESSMENT CRITERIA – QUESTIONS TO CONSIDER

1   Can the children use the apparatus to balance in a variety of ways?
2   Can the children transfer their weight from one body part to another?
3   Are they able to describe how they feel after activity?
4   Are they able to name one or two muscle groups in the arms, for example triceps and biceps?

Sessions 10 and 11

Travelling – on large parts (emphasis on sliding)

Consolidation from previous session: to perform balances, wholly on the apparatus, touching more than one piece of apparatus, touching the floor and apparatus, and balancing away from the apparatus.

LEARNING OBJECTIVES

(The objectives of the session need to be made explicit to the children. They also need to assess the extent to which they have achieved them.)

Physical

1   To know how to perform sliding actions using the body to push and pull.
2   To replicate a sequence that includes a range of balances with sliding actions.

Well-being

3   To identify what is good in a peer's performance and be able to communicate this in a positive manner.

Broader learning

4   To revise naming particular muscle groups (arms and/or legs).

ASSESSMENT CRITERIA – QUESTIONS TO CONSIDER

1   Can the children perform a sliding action by pushing and/or pulling?
2   Can they replicate a sequence that includes different balances and sliding actions?
3   Can children observe each other and give positive, supportive feedback?
4   Are they able to remember one or two muscle groups, for example biceps, triceps, hamstring, quadriceps and calf?

Sessions 12 and 13

Travelling – on large parts (emphasis on rolling)

Consolidation from previous session: to incorporate balances and sliding actions using the body to push and pull.

LEARNING OBJECTIVES

(The objectives of the session need to be made explicit to the children. They also need to assess the extent to which they have achieved them.)

Physical

1   To know how to perform a variety of rolls.
2   To adapt a sequence from the floor to the apparatus.

Well-being

3   To know that being strong and supple are vital attributes for effective gymnastic performances.

Broader learning

4   To negotiate and collaborate in order to devise a sequence of movements.

ASSESSMENT CRITERIA – QUESTIONS TO CONSIDER

1   Can the children perform the following rolls: log, one leg leading, teddy bear, sideways shoulder, tuck and stretch?
2   Can they adapt their sequence from the floor to the apparatus?
3   Can the children name the key physical attributes that they need to develop in order to perform effectively in gymnastics?
4   Are they able to share ideas, show their movements to one another and negotiate which movements to select to form a sequence?

Sessions 14 and 15

Travelling – introducing forward roll

(See 'Specific skills guide' – Forward roll, page 218.)

Consolidation from previous session: to consolidate the following rolls: log roll, one leg leading, teddy bear, sideways shoulder, tuck and stretch.

LEARNING OBJECTIVES

(The objectives of the session need to be made explicit to the children. They also need to assess the extent to which they have achieved them.)

Physical

1   To learn how to perform a correct and safe forward roll.
2   To use criteria to improve performance.

Well-being

3   To know that being strong and supple are vital attributes for effective gymnastic performances.

Broader learning

4   To identify muscle groups that are important in activity.

ASSESSMENT CRITERIA – QUESTIONS TO CONSIDER

1   Can the children begin to perform a correct and safe forward roll?
2   Are they able to assess their work against criteria, making adjustments that show improvement?
3   Can the children name the key attributes that they need to develop in order to perform effectively in gymnastics?
4   Are they able to name one or two muscle groups discussed in earlier sessions?

Sessions 16 and 17

Jumping

(See 'Specific skills guide' – Jumping, page 216.)

Consolidation from previous session: to learn to perform the forward roll.

LEARNING OBJECTIVES

(The objectives of the session need to be made explicit to the children. They also need to assess the extent to which they have achieved them.)

Physical

1   To know how to perform a variety of jumps.
2   To use criteria to improve performance.

Well-being

3   To know some activities that will develop strength and suppleness.

Broader learning

4   To relate knowledge of 'degrees' in performing turning jumps.

ASSESSMENT CRITERIA – QUESTIONS TO CONSIDER

1   Can the children perform the following jumps: straight, star, scissor etc.?
2   Can the children assess each other's movements against given criteria and then improve their performances?
3   Are they able to suggest and perform activities that develop strength and suppleness?
4   Can they relate their knowledge of 'degrees' in performing turning jumps?

Sessions 18 and 19

Jumping, balancing and travelling

Consolidation from previous session: to combine a variety of jumps in a sequence that includes straight, star, scissor and turning jumps performed at 45°, 90°, 180° and 360°.

LEARNING OBJECTIVES

(The objectives of the session need to be made explicit to the children. They also need to assess the extent to which they have achieved them.)

Physical

1   To know how to perform a variety of jumps, balances and travelling actions.
2   To know how to link contrasting movements smoothly.

Well-being

3   To be able to suggest warm-up activities.

Broader learning

4   To compare and contrast actions identifying similarities and differences.

ASSESSMENT CRITERIA – QUESTIONS TO CONSIDER

1   Can the children perform a variety of jumps, balances and travelling actions?
2   Do the children link contrasting actions smoothly?
3   Are the children able to suggest and perform suitable warm-up activities?
4   Are the children able to watch others and identify similarities and differences in another's movements?

Session 20

Assessment activity

This session will assess children's knowledge and understanding gained from the sessions throughout the year. Children should be encouraged to take responsibility for their own learning by identifying what they can achieve, what they need to do to develop and how they will do this.

LEARNING OBJECTIVES

(The objectives of the session need to be made explicit to the children. They also need to assess the extent to which they have achieved them.)

Physical

1 To perform a sequence of contrasting actions.
2 To adapt a sequence performed on the floor to include both the floor and apparatus.
3 To remember and perform the sequence with consistency, coordination and control.

Well-being

4 To know that strength and suppleness are key attributes of a gymnast.

Broader learning

5 To identify actions and movements that they can perform well, and know one or two ways in which to improve.

DISCUSSION

Discuss and share ideas of the key attributes of a gymnast and why being strong and supple is important.

Talk about what constitutes good work and how improvements can be made.

ASSESSMENT CRITERIA – QUESTIONS TO CONSIDER

1 Can the children perform contrasting actions in a sequence?
2 Can they adapt their sequence from the floor to include both the floor and apparatus?
3 Can they remember and perform the sequence with consistency, coordination and control?
4 Can the children talk about what a gymnast needs to develop physically and so improve their performance?
5 Can they identify actions and movements that they can perform well, and know one or two ways in which they can improve?

OUTCOME

Some children will achieve, some will excel and some will achieve less.

Overall plan

Year 4

Session 1

Assessment activity

This first session is for an initial assessment of the children's capabilities to ascertain what they know and what they can do.

This session relates, in part, to the final assessment task in Year 3.

LEARNING OBJECTIVES

(The objectives of the session need to be made explicit to the children. They also need to assess the extent to which they have achieved them.)

Physical

1   To perform a sequence of contrasting actions.
2   To adapt a sequence performed on the floor to include both the floor and apparatus.
3   To remember and perform the sequence with consistency, coordination and control.

Well-being

4   To know that strength and suppleness are key attributes of a gymnast.

Broader learning

5   To identify actions and movements that they can perform well, and know one or two ways in which to improve.

DISCUSSION

Discuss and share ideas of the key attributes of a gymnast and why being strong and supple is important.

Talk about what constitutes good work and how improvements can be made.

ASSESSMENT CRITERIA – QUESTIONS TO CONSIDER

1   Can the children perform contrasting actions in a sequence?

2   Can they adapt their sequence from the floor to include both the floor and apparatus?

3   Can they remember and perform the sequence with consistency, coordination and control?

4   Can the children talk about what a gymnast needs to develop physically and so improve their performance?

5   Are they able to identify actions and movements that they can perform well, and know one or two ways in which they can improve?

OUTCOME

Some children will achieve, some will excel and some will achieve less.

Sessions 2 and 3

Travelling – jumping and rolling

Consolidation from previous session: this session directs the children's attention quite specifically towards improving the skill of jumping and rolling in a variety of ways, allowing them to consolidate previously learned skills and develop new ones.

LEARNING OBJECTIVES

(The objectives of the session need to be made explicit to the children. They also need to assess the extent to which they have achieved them.)

Physical

1   To continue to develop performance in a variety of jumps and rolls.
2   To use criteria to improve their and others' performances.

Well-being

3   To articulate the kinds of activity that will develop their strength and suppleness.

Broader learning

4   To be able to plan the timing of actions with their partners.

ASSESSMENT CRITERIA – QUESTIONS TO CONSIDER

1   Can the children perform a variety of jumps and rolls with control and coordination?
2   Can the children assess their own and others' performances against given criteria?
3   Can children suggest and perform activities that develop their strength and suppleness?
4   Within a sequence are the children able to perform actions in unison?

Sessions 4 and 5

Travelling – jumping and rolling

Consolidation from previous session: in pairs to perform a variety of jumping and rolling actions in a sequence, with one jump being performed in unison; and to adapt the sequence on to both floor and apparatus.

LEARNING OBJECTIVES

(The objectives of the session need to be made explicit to the children. They also need to assess the extent to which they have achieved them.)

Physical

1   To learn how to perform a correct and safe backward roll.
2   To use criteria to improve performance.

Well-being

3   To be able to communicate ideas to another.

Broader learning

4   To be able to explore a range of ideas.

ASSESSMENT CRITERIA – QUESTIONS TO CONSIDER

1   Can the children perform a correct and safe backward roll?
2   Are they able to assess their and others' work against criteria, making adjustments to show improvement?
3   Can the children communicate effectively and share ideas to achieve an ultimate performance?
4   Are the children willing to try a variety of body shapes to develop their work?

Sessions 6 and 7

Balance – with travelling into and out of balance, and introducing headstand

(See 'Specific skills guide' – Headstand, page 221.)
Consolidation from previous session: to revise and continue to learn forward and backward rolls.

LEARNING OBJECTIVES

(The objectives of the session need to be made explicit to the children. They also need to assess the extent to which they have achieved them.)

Physical

1   To learn to perform a correct and safe headstand.
2   To understand the terms mirror, match, canon and unison when working with a partner.

Well-being

3   To add to the range of activities that will develop strength and suppleness.

Broader learning

4   To know what a ¼, ½, ¾ and whole turn are in degrees.

ASSESSMENT CRITERIA – QUESTIONS TO CONSIDER

1   Can the children perform a correct and safe headstand?
2   Are they able to work with a partner showing mirroring, matching and working in canon and unison – and can they identify the different actions?
3   Can they suggest and perform activities that develop their strength and suppleness?
4   Are they able to perform a ¼, ½, ¾ and whole turn and know the equivalent in degrees?

Sessions 8 and 9

Travelling – achieving variety using body shape and speed emphasis

Consolidation from previous session: travelling into and out of balance using rolls and jumps learned in previous sessions – and performing a headstand.

LEARNING OBJECTIVES

(The objectives of the session need to be made explicit to the children. They also need to assess the extent to which they have achieved them.)

Physical

1   To learn to perform a movement varying the body shape and assess what might occur.
2   To understand that some movements have natural fast speeds and others slow.

Well-being

3   To articulate the changes that happen to the body during activity, and the benefits to health and well-being of being active.

Broader learning

4   To remember and name muscle groups.

ASSESSMENT CRITERIA – QUESTIONS TO CONSIDER

1   Can the children perform the same movement with various body shapes and then assess what might occur (for example a tucked, extended, feet apart, feet together, roll etc.)?
2   Can they recognise that a jump is a naturally fast action whereas a balance is more pleasing for an audience when performed in a controlled slow manner?
3   Can the children talk about the changes that happen to their bodies when they are active and identify some benefits to their health and well-being?
4   Are they able to remember and name muscle groups?

Sessions 14 and 15

Travelling and balance

Consolidation from previous session: combining taking weight on the hands, jumps, rolls and balance in a sequence that includes changes in levels, direction and speed, and may include performing a handstand.

LEARNING OBJECTIVES

(The objectives of the session need to be made explicit to the children. They also need to assess the extent to which they have achieved them.)

Physical

1   To know how to change body shape within actions to add variety to a sequence.
2   To know why it is important to warm up prior to activity and how to do so.

Well-being

3   To know some of the muscles that need to be strong and supple in order to optimise gymnastic performance.

Broader learning

4   To use gymnastic terms to describe body shapes.

ASSESSMENT CRITERIA – QUESTIONS TO CONSIDER

1   Can the children change their body shapes within actions in their sequences?
2   Are they able to lead a partner through a short warm-up and understand why they are doing so?
3   Can they identify one or two muscles groups that need to be strong to maximise gymnastic performance?
4   Can the children use gymnastic vocabulary to describe each other's body shapes, for example tucked, extended, stretched, arched and piked?

Sessions 16 and 17

Springing and landing with rotation

Consolidation from previous session: to add variety to a sequence by changing body shape.

LEARNING OBJECTIVES

(The objectives of the session need to be made explicit to the children. They also need to assess the extent to which they have achieved them.)

Physical

1   To know how to rotate jumping actions.
2   To consolidate springing and jumping on to and off the apparatus.

Well-being

3   To know about activities that will develop their strength and suppleness.

Broader learning

4   To know that a healthy diet, adequate sleep and other factors are important in optimising sporting achievement.

ASSESSMENT CRITERIA – QUESTIONS TO CONSIDER

1   Are the children able to perform a sequence that includes jumps with rotation?
2   Can they demonstrate springing and jumping actions on to and off the apparatus?
3   Can the children suggest and perform activities that develop their strength and suppleness?
4   Are they able to name some key lifestyle considerations in achieving sporting success?

Sessions 18 and 19

Rotation – cartwheels and different kinds of turning actions

(See 'Specific skills guide' – Cartwheel, page 225.)

Consolidation from previous session: to explore rotational movements and flight (by pushing off the apparatus with hands) and performing with a partner in unison.

LEARNING OBJECTIVES

(The objectives of the session need to be made explicit to the children. They also need to assess the extent to which they have achieved them.)

Physical

1   To learn to perform a correct and safe cartwheel.
2   To know why it is important to warm up prior to activity and how to do so.

Well-being

3   To identify which joint(s) are affected by different stretches.

Broader learning

4   To share ideas and support one another in an encouraging, constructive way.

ASSESSMENT CRITERIA – QUESTIONS TO CONSIDER

1   Can children perform a correct and safe cartwheel?
2   Are they able to lead a partner through a short warm-up and understand why they are doing so?
3   Can the children name joints that are affected by different stretches, for example elbow, shoulder, ankle etc.?
4   Can they share ideas when planning sequences? Are they supportive when watching each other's performances, giving positive and constructive feedback?

Session 20

Assessment activity

This session will assess children's knowledge and understanding gained from the sessions throughout the year. Children should be encouraged to take responsibility for their own learning by identifying what they can achieve, what they need to do to develop and how they will do this.

LEARNING OBJECTIVES

(The objectives of the session need to be made explicit to the children. They also need to assess the extent to which they have achieved them.)

Physical

1   To perform a sequence of contrasting actions.
2   To adapt a sequence performed on the floor to include both the floor and apparatus.
3   To remember and perform the sequence with consistency, coordination and control.

Well-being

4   To know that strength and suppleness are key attributes of a gymnast.

Broader learning

5   To know how to adapt actions to accommodate individual abilities.

DISCUSSION

Discuss and share ideas of the key attributes of a gymnast and why being strong and supple is important.

Talk about what constitutes good work and how improvements can be made.

ASSESSMENT CRITERIA – QUESTIONS TO CONSIDER

1   Can the children perform contrasting actions in a sequence?
2   Can they adapt their sequence from the floor to include both the floor and apparatus?
3   Can they remember and perform the sequence with consistency, coordination and control?
4   Can the children talk about what a gymnast needs to develop physically and so improve their performance?
5   Can they adapt actions within their sequence to accommodate their individual abilities?

OUTCOME

Some children will achieve, some will excel and some will achieve less.

Overall plan
Year 5

Session 1

Assessment activity

This first session is for an initial assessment of the children's capabilities to ascertain what they know and what they can do.

This session relates to the final assessment task in Year 4.

LEARNING OBJECTIVES

(The objectives of the session need to be made explicit to the children. They also need to assess the extent to which they have achieved them.)

Physical

1   To perform a sequence of contrasting actions.
2   To adapt a sequence performed on the floor to include both the floor and apparatus.
3   To remember and perform the sequence with consistency, coordination and control.

Well-being

4   To know that strength and suppleness are key attributes of a gymnast.

Broader learning

5   To know how to adapt actions to accommodate individual abilities.

DISCUSSION

Discuss and share ideas of the key attributes of a gymnast and why being strong and supple is important.

Talk about what constitutes good work and how improvements can be made.

ASSESSMENT CRITERIA – QUESTIONS TO CONSIDER

1 Can the children perform contrasting actions in a sequence?

2 Can they adapt their sequence from the floor to include both the floor and apparatus?

3 Can they remember and perform the sequence with consistency, coordination and control?

4 Can the children talk about what a gymnast needs to develop physically and so improve their performance?

5 Can they adapt actions within their sequence to accommodate their individual abilities?

OUTCOME

Some children will achieve, some will excel and some will achieve less.

Sessions 2 and 3

Balance – counterbalance and counter-tension

Consolidation from previous session: to perform contrasting actions in a sequence that the children can replicate on both the floor and apparatus.

LEARNING OBJECTIVES

(The objectives of the session need to be made explicit to the children. They also need to assess the extent to which they have achieved them.)

Physical

1   To learn how to perform an action involving counter-tension with a partner.
2   To continue to develop an understanding of why it is important to warm up prior to activity and how to do so.

Well-being

3   To know further activities that develop strength and suppleness.

Broader learning

4   To be able to teach an action to another person.

ASSESSMENT CRITERIA – QUESTIONS TO CONSIDER

1   Can the children perform an action with their partner using counter-tension?
2   Are the children able to lead a partner through a short warm-up and understand why they are doing so?
3   Are they able, in pairs, to share ideas of actions that develop both suppleness and strength?
4   Can pairs teach their action with counter-tension to another pair?

Sessions 4 and 5

Balance – counterbalance and counter-tension combined with actions

Consolidation from previous session: to introduce performing an action with a partner involving counter-tension.

LEARNING OBJECTIVES

(The objectives of the session need to be made explicit to the children. They also need to assess the extent to which they have achieved them.)

Physical

1   To continue to learn how to perform an action involving counter-tension with a partner and learn about counterbalance.

2   To use criteria to improve their own and others' performances.

Well-being

3   To identify the changes that occur to their bodies during activity and know how this is beneficial to their health.

Broader learning

4   To be able to teach an action to another person.

ASSESSMENT CRITERIA – QUESTIONS TO CONSIDER

1   Can the children perform additional actions with counter-tension with their partner, and show they understand what counterbalance is?

2   Can the children assess their own and others' performances against given criteria?

3   Are they able to identify the changes that occur to their bodies during activity and describe how this is beneficial to their health?

4   Can pairs teach their action involving counterbalance/-tension to another pair?

Sessions 6 and 7

Rotation – turning into and out of balance

Consolidation from previous session: to combine actions with counterbalance and counter-tension on both the floor and apparatus.

LEARNING OBJECTIVES

(The objectives of the session need to be made explicit to the children. They also need to assess the extent to which they have achieved them.)

Physical

1   To revise moving into and out of balance with turning (learning about axes of rotation).
2   To know that accuracy, consistency and clarity of movement are key to successful performance.

Well-being

3   To identify which joints are affected by different stretches.

Broader learning

4   To share ideas and support one another in an encouraging, constructive way.

ASSESSMENT CRITERIA – QUESTIONS TO CONSIDER

1   Can the children perform controlled balances from and into other movements using turns, and do they know which axis they are turning around?
2   Can the children work on accuracy, consistency and clarity of movement in their sequence?
3   Are they able to name joints that are affected by different stretches, for example elbow, shoulder, ankle etc.?
4   Can children share ideas when planning sequences and be supportive when watching others' performances, giving positive and constructive feedback?

Sessions 8 and 9

Performance preparation

Consolidation from previous session: to work on sequences that include moving into and out of balance, and into jumps and rolls.

LEARNING OBJECTIVES

(The objectives of the session need to be made explicit to the children. They also need to assess the extent to which they have achieved them.)

Physical

1   To develop a sequence against given criteria where the children choose to work on the floor or apparatus.
2   To know that accuracy, consistency and clarity of movement are key to successful performances.

Well-being

3   To identify some health and safety issues, for example the importance of wearing correct clothing, no jewellery, of having hair tied back, of there being no obstructions in the hall, of being aware of others in the space, etc.

Broader learning

4   To evaluate each other's performances against given criteria and give feedback in a positive and constructive way.

ASSESSMENT CRITERIA – QUESTIONS TO CONSIDER

1   Can the children use criteria to develop their sequence, choosing the floor or apparatus?
2   Can they work on accuracy, consistency and clarity of movement in their sequences?
3   Are they able to verbalise some health and safety issues that they need to be aware of in gymnastics?
4   Are they able to use criteria to evaluate each other's performances and give positive and constructive feedback?

Sessions 10 and 11

Springing and landing – introducing 'round-off'

(See 'Specific skills guide' – Round-off, page 226.)

Consolidation from previous session: performing a sequence as if to an audience that includes balancing into and out of jumps, rolls and actions performed with various body shapes.

LEARNING OBJECTIVES

(The objectives of the session need to be made explicit to the children. They also need to assess the extent to which they have achieved them.)

Physical

1   To learn how to 'round off' a cartwheel action.
2   To learn a range of springing actions using the apparatus, emphasising the flight phase.

Well-being

3   To gain an understanding of how muscles work.

Broader learning

4   To use given criteria to develop their work.

ASSESSMENT CRITERIA – QUESTIONS TO CONSIDER

1   Can the children 'round off' a cartwheel action?
2   Can they perform a range of actions on the apparatus that emphasise the springing and/or flight phase?
3   Are they able to describe how the muscles shorten when they are working and lengthen when relaxed?
4   Can they use given criteria to develop their work?

Sessions 12 and 13

Travelling – with bridging

Consolidation from previous session: to learn springing and landing actions, and the 'round-off'.

LEARNING OBJECTIVES

(The objectives of the session need to be made explicit to the children. They also need to assess the extent to which they have achieved them.)

Physical

1   To learn how to make a bridged body shape on the floor and apparatus.
2   To work in a variety of ways with a partner.

Well-being

3   To use space effectively for working safely on the apparatus.

Broader learning

4   To copy another's sequence.

ASSESSMENT CRITERIA – QUESTIONS TO CONSIDER

1   Can the children make a variety of bridged body shapes and hold them with strong body tension?
2   Are they able to work in a variety of ways with a partner that includes counterbalance/-tension, matching, mirroring and working in canon?
3   Can the children move between apparatus safely avoiding others?
4   Can the children copy their partner's sequence consistently and accurately?

Sessions 14 and 15

Emphasising symmetry and asymmetry

Consolidation from previous session: to make bridged body shapes and combine with actions on, across and off apparatus.

LEARNING OBJECTIVES

(The objectives of the session need to be made explicit to the children. They also need to assess the extent to which they have achieved them.)

Physical

1 To understand the difference between symmetrical and asymmetrical movements.
2 To plan and perform a sequence consistently and with control.

Well-being

3 To know some activities that stretch and strengthen muscles and joints.

Broader learning

4 To be able to teach movements and actions to others.

ASSESSMENT CRITERIA – QUESTIONS TO CONSIDER

1 Can the children perform symmetrical and asymmetrical movements when instructed?
2 Can they plan a sequence independently where actions and movements are controlled and consistent?
3 Can they share and perform exercises that strengthen and stretch muscles and joints?
4 In pairs, can the children teach their sequence to another pair?

Sessions 16 and 17

Action phrases – emphasising symmetry and asymmetry (on apparatus)

Consolidation from previous session: to explore actions with symmetry and asymmetry.

LEARNING OBJECTIVES

(The objectives of the session need to be made explicit to the children. They also need to assess the extent to which they have achieved them.)

Physical

1   To adapt actions that have symmetrical and asymmetrical shapes on to the apparatus.
2   To plan and perform a sequence consistently and with control.

Well-being

3   To know some activities that stretch and strengthen muscles and joints.

Broader learning

4   To use given criteria to develop the work.

ASSESSMENT CRITERIA – QUESTIONS TO CONSIDER

1   Can the children adapt actions that have symmetrical and asymmetrical shapes on to the apparatus?
2   Can they plan a sequence independently where actions are controlled and performed with clarity?
3   Can they identify activities that stretch and strengthen muscles and joints?
4   Are they able to use given criteria to develop their work?

Sessions 18 and 19

Preparation for performance combining actions previously learned

Consolidation from previous session: to adapt actions that are symmetrical and asymmetrical from the floor on to the apparatus.

LEARNING OBJECTIVES

(The objectives of the session need to be made explicit to the children. They also need to assess the extent to which they have achieved them.)

Physical

1   To revise previously learned actions, for example bridging, counter-tension, counterbalance, cartwheels, round-off etc., and include them in a sequence.
2   To know that accuracy, consistency and clarity of movement are key to successful performances.

Well-being

3   To identify which joints are affected by different stretches.

Broader learning

4   To share ideas and support one another in an encouraging, constructive way.

ASSESSMENT CRITERIA – QUESTIONS TO CONSIDER

1   Do the children use previously learned actions in their sequences?
2   Do they know that accuracy, consistency and clarity of movement are key to successful performances?
3   Are they able to name joints that are affected by different stretches, for example elbow, shoulder, ankle etc.?
4   Can children share ideas when planning sequences, and be supportive when watching others' performances, giving positive and constructive feedback?

Session 20

Assessment activity

This session will assess children's knowledge and understanding gained from the sessions throughout the year. Children should be encouraged to take responsibility for their own learning by identifying what they can achieve, what they need to do to develop and how they will do this.

LEARNING OBJECTIVES

(The objectives of the session need to be made explicit to the children. They also need to assess the extent to which they have achieved them.)

Physical

1 To perform a sequence of contrasting actions.
2 To adapt a sequence performed on the floor to include both the floor and apparatus.
3 To remember and perform the sequence with consistency, coordination and control.

Well-being

4 To know that strength and suppleness are key attributes of a gymnast.

Broader learning

5 To know how to adapt actions to accommodate individual abilities.

DISCUSSION

Discuss and share ideas of the key attributes of a gymnast and why being strong and supple is important.

Talk about what constitutes good work and how improvements can be made.

ASSESSMENT CRITERIA – QUESTIONS TO CONSIDER

1   Can the children perform contrasting actions in a sequence?

2   Can they adapt their sequence from the floor to include both the floor and apparatus?

3   Can they remember and perform the sequence with consistency, coordination and control?

4   Can the children talk about what a gymnast needs to develop physically and so improve their performance?

5   Can they adapt actions within their sequence to accommodate their individual abilities?

OUTCOME

Some children will achieve, some will excel and some will achieve less.

Overall plan
Year 6

Session 1

Assessment activity

This first session is for an initial assessment of the children's capabilities to ascertain what they know and what they can do.

This session relates to the final assessment task in Year 5.

LEARNING OBJECTIVES

(The objectives of the session need to be made explicit to the children. They also need to assess the extent to which they have achieved them.)

Physical

1 To perform a sequence of contrasting actions.
2 To adapt a sequence performed on the floor to include both the floor and apparatus.
3 To remember and perform the sequence with consistency, coordination and control.

Well-being

4 To know that strength and suppleness are key attributes of a gymnast.

Broader learning

5 To know how to adapt actions to accommodate individual abilities.

DISCUSSION

Discuss and share ideas of the key attributes of a gymnast and why being strong and supple is important.

Talk about what constitutes good work and how improvements can be made.

ASSESSMENT CRITERIA – QUESTIONS TO CONSIDER

1   Can the children perform contrasting actions in a sequence?

2   Can they adapt their sequence from the floor to include both the floor and apparatus?

3   Can they remember and perform the sequence with consistency, coordination and control?

4   Can the children talk about what a gymnast needs to develop physically and so improve their performance?

5   Can they adapt actions within their sequence to accommodate their individual abilities?

OUTCOME

Some children will achieve, some will excel and some will achieve less.

Sessions 2 and 3

Rotation – twisting and turning

Consolidation from previous session: to perform a sequence with a partner that includes the following actions: counterbalance, counter-tension, bridging and cartwheel with round-off landing.

LEARNING OBJECTIVES

(The objectives of the session need to be made explicit to the children. They also need to assess the extent to which they have achieved them.)

Physical

1   To perform twisting and rotating actions that lead into another action.
2   To know a variety of body parts that can be used as a base for a rotating and/or twisting action.

Well-being

3   To know why it is important to warm up prior to activity and how to do so.

Broader learning

4   To work safely in a space.

ASSESSMENT CRITERIA – QUESTIONS TO CONSIDER

1   Can children perform a twisting and rotating action that leads into a jump, roll etc.?
2   Can children use a variety of body parts to support rotating or twisting actions?
3   Can the children lead a warm-up with a small group of their peers, showing that they understand the importance of being prepared for activity?
4   Are the children aware of others and equipment when they travel around the hall?

Sessions 4 and 5

Rotation – twisting and turning on the apparatus

(A CD player, iPod station or similar will be needed for this session.)

Consolidation from previous session: to perform twisting and turning actions using a variety of body parts as a base, in pairs and small groups.

LEARNING OBJECTIVES

(The objectives of the session need to be made explicit to the children. They also need to assess the extent to which they have achieved them.)

Physical

1   To perform twisting and rotating actions that lead into another action both on the floor and apparatus, and to begin to work with music.
2   To perform actions in a sequence with varied speeds.

Well-being

3   To know why it is important to warm up prior to activity and how to do so.

Broader learning

4   To use given criteria to develop movements and improve performance.

ASSESSMENT CRITERIA – QUESTIONS TO CONSIDER

1   Can children perform a twisting and rotating action that leads into a jump, roll etc. both on the floor and apparatus, and begin to work with music?
2   Can children perform actions in a sequence with contrasting speed?
3   Can the children lead a warm-up with a small group of their peers, showing that they understand the importance of being prepared for activity?
4   Can the children use given criteria to develop movements and improve performance?

Sessions 6 and 7

Partner work relating to turning into and out of balance with travel

Consolidation from previous session: to perform twisting and turning actions using a variety of body parts as a base on the apparatus, in pairs and small groups.

LEARNING OBJECTIVES

(The objectives of the session need to be made explicit to the children. They also need to assess the extent to which they have achieved them.)

Physical

1   To negotiate obstacles when performing actions.
2   To know how to time actions to work successfully with a partner.

Well-being

3   To identify which joints are affected by different stretches.

Broader learning

4   To assess each other's skills and plan a sequence accordingly.

ASSESSMENT CRITERIA – QUESTIONS TO CONSIDER

1   Are the children able to plan and perform actions where they use each other as obstacles and perform actions over, under or through etc.?
2   Can they time their actions to move safely and fluently with their partner in a sequence?
3   Are they able to name joints that are affected by different stretches, for example elbow, shoulder, ankle etc.?
4   Are they able to adapt their actions to cater for each other's ability?

Sessions 8 and 9

Partner work – contact with obstacles related to balance, and performance preparation

Consolidation from previous session: to work in pairs to perform actions using each other as obstacles (still and moving).

LEARNING OBJECTIVES

(The objectives of the session need to be made explicit to the children. They also need to assess the extent to which they have achieved them.)

Physical

1   To use an obstacle to balance against.
2   To be able to combine a range of actions in a sequence with control and consistency.

Well-being

3   To gain further understanding of how muscles work.

Broader learning

4   To assess each other's skills and plan a sequence accordingly.

ASSESSMENT CRITERIA – QUESTIONS TO CONSIDER

1   Can children use their partners to support their balance?
2   Can they replicate a sequence of actions that they have planned and that demonstrates strong body control?
3   Can children describe how muscles shorten when they are working together and lengthen when they relax?
4   Are they able to adapt their actions to cater for each other's ability?

Sessions 10 and 11

Performance preparation

Consolidation from previous session: to use obstacles for balancing, and to plan a sequence that includes previous Year 6 content.

LEARNING OBJECTIVES

(The objectives of the session need to be made explicit to the children. They also need to assess the extent to which they have achieved them.)

Physical

1   To develop a sequence against criteria to perform to an audience.
2   To know that accuracy, consistency and clarity of movement are key to successful performances.

Well-being

3   To know why warming up and cooling down are important.

Broader learning

4   To be able to negotiate, share ideas and work with others to devise a sequence of actions.

ASSESSMENT CRITERIA – QUESTIONS TO CONSIDER

1   Can the children use criteria to develop their sequence in preparation for performance?
2   Can they work on accuracy, consistency and clarity of movement in their sequences?
3   Are children aware of the benefits of warming up and cooling down before and after activity?
4   Can children negotiate, share ideas and work with others to plan a final performance?

Sessions 12 and 13

Further development of basic skills

Consolidation from previous session: to perform a group sequence consisting of using obstacles as support or to go over, under etc.; twisting and turning actions; travel and roll.

LEARNING OBJECTIVES

(The objectives of the session need to be made explicit to the children. They also need to assess the extent to which they have achieved them.)

Physical

1   To be able to develop actions against given criteria.
2   To know that accuracy, consistency and clarity of movement are key to successful performances.

Well-being

3   To understand how activity contributes to a healthy lifestyle.

Broader learning

4   To know how to give feedback in a positive and constructive manner.

ASSESSMENT CRITERIA – QUESTIONS TO CONSIDER

1   Can the children use criteria to develop their actions?
2   Can they work on accuracy, consistency and clarity of movement in their sequences?
3   Can children describe some ways in which activity will support their lifestyle?
4   Do children feed back in a positive and constructive manner to one another?

Sessions 14 and 15

Revising previous actions – bridging, balancing, twisting, turning, springing, and symmetrical and asymmetrical body shapes, with a partner and in groups

(A CD player, iPod station or similar will be needed for this session.)

Consolidation from previous session: to revise and further develop basic skills.

LEARNING OBJECTIVES

(The objectives of the session need to be made explicit to the children. They also need to assess the extent to which they have achieved them.)

Physical

1   To know a range of compositional principles to improve performance, for example level, direction and speed, mirroring, matching and working in unison and canon.
2   To be able to combine a range of actions in a sequence with control and consistency.

Well-being

3   To know how to prepare the body for gymnastics.

Broader learning

4   To compose a sequence so that it reflects the beat of the music.

ASSESSMENT CRITERIA – QUESTIONS TO CONSIDER

1 Do the children include a range of compositional principles to improve performance, for example level, direction and speed, mirroring and matching, and working in unison and canon?

2 Can they replicate a sequence of actions that they have planned and that demonstrates strong body control?

3 Are they able to perform activities that prepare the body for gymnastics?

4 Can they time their actions, working with the music?

Sessions 16 and 17

Revising previous actions and performing them on apparatus, and emphasising contrasts in speed, shape and levels

(A CD player, iPod station or similar will be needed for this session.)

Consolidation from previous session: to perform a group sequence that includes one or more of the following actions: balance, roll, jump, bridge, and an action where weight is transferred to the hands.

LEARNING OBJECTIVES

(The objectives of the session need to be made explicit to the children. They also need to assess the extent to which they have achieved them.)

Physical

1   To know a range of compositional principles to improve performance using the apparatus, for example contrasting speed, shape and levels.
2   To be able to combine a range of actions in a sequence with control and consistency.

Well-being

3   To articulate how activity contributes to a healthy lifestyle.

Broader learning

4   To compose a sequence so that it reflects the beat of the music.

ASSESSMENT CRITERIA – QUESTIONS TO CONSIDER

1   Do the children show contrasting speed, shape and levels in their performance on the apparatus?

2   Can they replicate a sequence of actions that they have planned and that demonstrates strong body control?

3   Can children describe some ways in which activity will support their lifestyle?

4   Can they time their actions, working with the music?

Sessions 18 and 19

Performance preparation

(A CD player, iPod station or similar will be needed for this session.)

Consolidation from previous session: to perform actions on the apparatus, emphasising contrasts in speed, shape and levels.

LEARNING OBJECTIVES

(The objectives of the session need to be made explicit to the children. They also need to assess the extent to which they have achieved them.)

Physical

1   To be able to devise a sequence responding to a given task.
2   To be able to combine a range of actions in a sequence with control and consistency.

Well-being

3   To articulate how activity contributes to a healthy lifestyle.

Broader learning

4   To assess each other's skills and abilities and plan a sequence accordingly.

ASSESSMENT CRITERIA – QUESTIONS TO CONSIDER

1   Do the children achieve up to eight to ten elements in their final performance?
2   Does their work demonstrate strong body control?
3   Can children describe some ways in which activity will support their lifestyle?
4   Are they able to adapt actions to cater for each other's ability?

Session 20

Assessment activity

(A CD player, iPod station or similar will be needed for this session.)

This session will assess children's knowledge and understanding gained from the sessions throughout the year. Children should be encouraged to take responsibility for their own learning by identifying what they can achieve, what they need to do to develop and how they will do this.

LEARNING OBJECTIVES

(The objectives of the session need to be made explicit to the children. They also need to assess the extent to which they have achieved them.)

Physical

1 To perform a sequence of contrasting actions in groups.
2 To adapt the sequence performed on the floor to include both the floor and apparatus.
3 To remember and perform the sequence with consistency, coordination and control.

Well-being

4 To know that strength and suppleness are key attributes of a gymnast.

Broader learning

5 To compose their sequence so it reflects the beat of the music.

DISCUSSION

Discuss and share ideas of the key attributes of a gymnast and why being strong and supple is important.

Talk about what constitutes good work and how improvements can be made.

ASSESSMENT CRITERIA – QUESTIONS TO CONSIDER

1 Can the children, in groups, perform contrasting actions in a sequence?
2 Can they adapt their sequence from the floor to include both the floor and apparatus?
3 Can they remember and perform the sequence with consistency, coordination and control?
4 Can the children talk about what a gymnast needs to develop physically and so improve their performance?
5 Can they time their actions, working with the music?

OUTCOME

Some children will achieve, some will excel and some will achieve less.

The sessions

Year 3

SESSION 1
Assessment activity

This first session is for an initial assessment of the children's capabilities to ascertain what they know and what they can do. It has only floor work.

This session relates, in part, to the final assessment tasks in Key Stage 1.

LEARNING OBJECTIVES

(The objectives of the session need to be made explicit to the children. They also need to assess the extent to which they have achieved them.)

Physical

1   To perform three travelling actions in a sequence.

2   To add a starting shape and a rotation action to complete the sequence.

3   To remember and perform the sequence with consistency, coordination and control.

Well-being

4   To articulate the changes happening to the body during activity, and the benefits of being active to health and well-being.

Broader learning

5   To identify actions and movements that they can perform well, and know one or two ways in which to improve.

DISCUSSION

Share ideas about what contributes to staying healthy and well.

Talk about what constitutes good work and how improvements can be made.

ASSESSMENT CRITERIA – QUESTIONS TO CONSIDER

1   Can the children perform three travelling actions in a sequence?

2   Can they add a starting shape and a rotation action to complete their sequence?

3   Can they remember and perform the sequence with consistency, coordination and control?

4   Can the children talk about the changes happening to their bodies when they are active and the benefits of being active to their health and well-being?

5   Can they identify actions and movements that they can perform well, and know one or two ways in which they can improve?

OUTCOME

Some children will achieve, some will excel and some will achieve less.

Warm-up

	Content	Teaching points
1	Play the Bean Game – children move around the hall according to the bean that is called out: runner bean – running; jumping bean – jumping; chilli bean – rubbing all body parts to keep warm; jelly bean – wobbling like jelly; frozen bean – being still; baked bean – lying down as if looking at the sky; butter bean – sliding on your bottom.	Verbalise the children's body actions and highlight where they are demonstrating with good control and tension.

Floor work

	Content	Teaching points
1	Select a starting position and on the sound of the tambour add two travelling actions to make a sequence.	Encourage the children to perform several different travelling actions and verbalise these. Encourage them to perform each travelling action for the count of three. Highlight clear starting positions.
2	Practise and refine, and when you can remember your sequence add another travelling action to it.	Circulate and set differentiated challenges to accommodate individual abilities.
3	Add a rotation/turning action to finish the sequence.	Select some children to show and draw attention to the variety of turning actions shown. Ask children what they can do well and what they need to do to improve.
4	Consider how you are going to finish your sequence. There should be a clear ending after the final turning action.	Select some children to show and highlight previously performed actions.
5	In pairs name yourselves 1 and 2 – 2s are to show 1s their sequence and then change over.	Encourage children to identify whether their partner included three actions, a turning action and a clear ending. The children should now discuss what they did well and what they need to do to improve.
	ASSESSMENT – By the teacher (in conjunction with a teaching assistant where applicable), and also peer-assessment by the children. Use ICT to record as many performances as possible so the children can self-assess during the lesson and in the classroom. This can also be kept as a record of their achievement.	

Final activity

Walk around the room, stretch up high and curl up tightly. Wait to be tapped to line up (enrol some children to help).

Classroom

In discussion with their partner, children are to make a note of their sequences to use later, and identify what they thought they did well and what they need to do to improve for the next lesson.

Developing suppleness

SESSIONS 2 AND 3

Balance – what is balance?

Consolidation from previous session: to perform three travelling actions in a sequence and perform the sequence with consistency, coordination and control.

LEARNING OBJECTIVES

(The objectives of the session need to be made explicit to the children. They also need to assess the extent to which they have achieved them.)

Physical

1   To know how to balance on different parts of the body using tension and extension.

2   To combine balancing actions by transferring the weight smoothly from one body part to another.

Well-being

3   To know that strength and suppleness are important components of gymnastics.

Broader learning

4   To share ideas with a partner and select actions together to combine in a sequence.

ASSESSMENT CRITERIA – QUESTIONS TO CONSIDER

1   Can the children balance on a variety of body parts with well-held body tension, and with toes and fingers extended?

2   Can children move smoothly in taking weight from one body part to another?

3   Can the children identify physical elements that affect gymnastic performance?

4   Can the children work together to create a sequence using each other's ideas?

Warm-up

Over the two-week period you may want to follow the ideas below, but add changes of direction, speed and levels and/or add more than one balance.

	Content	Teaching points
1	Run in and out of each other and on the sound of the tambour change direction of the run.	Relaxed style; awareness of space; able to change direction with good control and coordination.
2	Run in and out of each other and on the sound of the tambour hold a high balance.	Select children to show – highlight strong body tension, extended fingers and toes, the range of ideas.

3	Jump in and out of each other and on the sound of the tambour hold a low balance.	Select children to show – highlight strong body tension, extended fingers and toes, the range of ideas.
4	Hop in and out of each other and on the sound of the tambour select whether your balance is high or low.	Verbalise responses.
	DEVELOPING SUPPLENESS – Sit with your legs straight in front. Gently press the trunk down to the legs (hold for a count of 20 and relax) – easy pressure. **DEVELOPING STRENGTH** – Stand up and hop on alternate legs ten times each. **QUESTION** – How do both these exercises aid gymnastic performances? (This question, relating to suppleness and strength, focuses the children's attention on their importance in gymnastics.)	

Floor work

	Content	Teaching points
1	In your own space try to find different body parts on which you can hold your weight and be still.	Point out that it is easier to hold a balance if there is a wider base of support. Articulate responses and select two or three children to show.
2	Select from the range of the children's responses and all try these.	Question children as to why they may be losing balance. (There may be too much forward momentum prior to holding the balance, which takes the centre of gravity outside the base of support.)
3	Children sit on the floor in a space. Ask the children which parts of their body are touching the floor (probably their bottom and two feet).	Encourage good posture.
4	Now take your feet and hands off the floor and balance on your bottom only.	Feel what the body has to do to keep the balance. Try to get a 'perched' feel. How many parts of the body are touching the floor?
5	Now balance on your bottom, slowly extending your legs to finish in a V-sit position.	Which parts of the body are tense? What helps you achieve this position?
6	With your partner plan, perform and adapt a sequence that links moving from 'bottom' to 'side' to 'stomach'. Clearly show balance on each part.	Emphasise slow controlled movement between balances. Extend the body away from the point of balance. The children should be able to perform and repeat a simple sequence of balances with control and coordination.

Apparatus

	Content	Teaching points
1	In your pairs plan, perform and adapt your sequence using the floor and apparatus.	Encourage extension of feet and hands, strong body tension and smooth transitions. Select one or two pairs to demonstrate in order to highlight this.
2	One pair is to watch another and identify good body tension, extensions and smooth transitions.	Encourage children to identify that strength and suppleness are vital physical attributes for 'good performance'.

Final activity

In front support position with feet still, walk the hands round the compass (developing arm strength). Sit on your bottom, slowly stretch out your legs and place them on the floor; stretch out your arms and place them on your knees; slowly curl into a tight ball and hold.

Then stretch out fully and hold the stretch.

Classroom

Children should make a note of their sequence with their partner to use later, and identify what they thought they did well and what they need to do to improve for the next lesson.

SESSIONS 4 AND 5

Balance – what is balance?

Consolidation from previous session: to combine balances on different parts of the body in a sequence on the floor and apparatus.

LEARNING OBJECTIVES

(The objectives of the session need to be made explicit to the children. They also need to assess the extent to which they have achieved them.)

Physical

1   To be able to link balances on small and large body parts.

2   To be able to work with a partner to produce a sequence that can be remembered and performed well.

Well-being

3   To know that muscular strength can be developed through physical activity.

Broader learning

4   To be able to negotiate with a partner to create and adapt a sequence.

ASSESSMENT CRITERIA – QUESTIONS TO CONSIDER

1   Can the children link balances held on small body parts smoothly with balances on large body parts and vice versa?

2   Can they work with a partner and perform a sequence that they have both remembered?

3   Can the children identify that being physically active helps strengthen their muscles and heart?

4   Can children work together with another to create a sequence using each other's ideas on the floor and apparatus?

Warm-up

	Content	Teaching points
1	Run in and out of each other and on the sound of the tambour balance on your bottom and extend into a 'V' body shape.	Highlight good extension (feet and hands), strong body tensions, clear 'V' body shapes.
2	Jump in and out of each other and on the sound of the tambour balance on your bottom and move into another balance.	Verbalise responses. Highlight controlled smooth transitions from feet to bottom.

3	Hop in and out of each other and on the sound of the tambour select three balances and move smoothly from one into the other.	Share responses. Select one or two children to show and articulate the smooth transitions.
4	Hold a starting position and on the sound of the tambour combine three balances, selecting one of the balances that you have just seen or not previously tried.	Encourage smooth transitions and strong body tension.

DEVELOPING SUPPLENESS – Sit, stretching your legs as wide as is comfortable, rock on to your back and gently press your legs wider (hands press inside of thighs; keep legs straight). Do some ankle bending and stretching (concentrate on good mobility).

QUESTIONS – What are we developing when we warm up (suppleness and muscle strength etc.)? How do we develop muscle strength?

Floor work

	Content	Teaching points
1	Find balances on small body parts.	Look for different numbers of parts touching the floor. What happens to the rest of the body? Stretch it away from the base and hold a clear position before you try another one. Select two or three children to show, and encourage the children to try each other's ideas.
2	Find balances on large body parts.	Verbalise responses and select one or two children to show. Highlight good body tension, and stretched fingers and toes. Allow the children to try each other's ideas.
3	Link two balances on small body parts with two on large body parts.	Encourage smooth transitions and strong body tension.
4	In pairs, share your balances with your partner and decide which ones to include in your sequence.	Encourage children to evaluate each other's movements and adapt to take account of each other's ability.
5	With your partner plan, perform and adapt a sequence that has a clear starting position and includes four balances.	Ensure the children have contrasting body shapes in their sequences. Do they need to change the order to ensure smooth transitions?
6	In pairs show another pair your sequence.	Children are to watch each other and feed back on good body tension, variety of body shapes and smooth transitions. How did you manage to ensure that the transition between balances was smooth?

Apparatus

	Content	Teaching points
1	In your pairs plan, perform and adapt your sequence using both the floor and the apparatus.	Encourage good body tension, variety of body shapes and smooth transitions. Verbalise responses and show one or two good examples.
2	One pair is to watch another and give constructive feedback.	Explain that it is important to be positive when giving feedback, so children should highlight what they like about each other's performances but also select one way in which they could improve (holding balances with strong body tension). Give children an opportunity to build this into their sequences.

Final activity

Squat jump around the room (explain that this strengthens the legs). Then stretch up high; slowly fold your body down so that you curl into a tight ball on the floor. Stretch out and hold the stretch for a count of 10.

Classroom

Children should make a note of their sequence with their partner to use later, and identify what they thought they did well and what they need to do to improve for the next lesson.

SESSIONS 6 AND 7
Balance – related to shape

Consolidation from previous session: to combine balances on small parts of the body with large part body balances.

LEARNING OBJECTIVES

(The objectives of the session need to be made explicit to the children. They also need to assess the extent to which they have achieved them.)

Physical

1   To be able to balance holding different body shapes.

2   To improve performance using particular criteria for evaluation.

Well-being

3   To know some of the benefits to health and well-being of physical activity.

Broader learning

4   To name particular muscle groups.

ASSESSMENT CRITERIA – QUESTIONS TO CONSIDER

1   Can the children perform balances holding stretched, tucked, narrow and wide shapes?

2   Can they explain what they have to do to improve their movements and then take action?

3   Can the children articulate some benefits of engaging in an active lifestyle?

4   Can they name one or two leg muscle groups, for example hamstring, quadriceps and calf?

Warm-up

	Content	Teaching points
1	Skip in and out of each other and on the sound of the tambour balance on a small body part.	Verbalise responses – look for smooth transitions between motion and stillness.
2	Run in and out of each other and on the sound of the tambour balance on a large body part.	Verbalise responses as above.
3	Run, skip, hop or jump and combine with a change of direction, speed and level. On one strike of the tambour balance on one body part; on two strikes, two body parts etc.	This may need to be broken down and then built back up again.

DEVELOPING SUPPLENESS – Sit with your legs straight in front. Gently press your trunk down to your legs (hold for a count of 20 and relax – easy pressure).

DEVELOPING STRENGTH – Take your weight on both hands and push your bottom and tucked legs into the air (five times).

QUESTIONS – Can the children name any muscles in the leg? Can they articulate some benefits of engaging in an active lifestyle?

Floor work

	Content	Teaching points
1	Balance on large parts of the body showing first a narrow stretched shape and then (on the same part) a wide stretched shape.	Does it feel different? Did you have to do anything else to hold the balance?
2	Repeat with less of the body on the floor (for example, one hip).	Again, what difference do you notice?
3	Begin balanced in a tucked shape, slowly stretch out from this position, then change to a different tucked shape.	Still try to feel 'perched' in each balance. Use your arms and legs to help you get into the last balance. Select one or two good examples to highlight the sense of being 'perched'.
4	Develop a pattern of three balances showing tucked, narrow and stretched, and wide shapes. Try to move smoothly between each balance.	Select one or two children to show, and highlight different bases, discussing the different ways children move between the balances.
5	In pairs, share ideas and devise a joint sequence to include a variety of shapes where you hold the balances. Plan, practise and refine in preparation for performance.	Select pairs to show (quarter of the class). Encourage the rest of the class to feed back stating what they liked about the performance and naming the body shapes in the balances that they could see in the performance. If time allows, give all the children the opportunity to show.

Apparatus

	Content	Teaching points
1	With your partner perform your sequence using both the floor and apparatus. You may need to adapt some of your movements to achieve this.	Encourage the range of balances. Emphasise good control and smooth transitions. Verbalise responses and show a good example. The children will need to consider: (a) holding/gripping parts of the apparatus, (b) stretching away from it, and (c) leaning against/balancing on/pulling away from it etc.
2	Pairs are to watch one another and peer-assess, giving positive feedback and using the given criteria.	Give children the opportunity to incorporate the feedback received into their sequences. Criteria will be: variety of body shapes, smooth transitions, strong body tension, and interesting use of the apparatus.

Final activity

Children should be in pairs 'duck fighting': in a crouched position facing each other. Children place their hands in front of their chests and try to unbalance each other using the flats of their hands. They must stay in a crouched position (leg strength).

Hold a one-point balance (balancing on one body part), move into a two-point, then a three-point and hold a four-point balance. Stand up and stretch up fully.

Classroom

Children should make a note of their sequence with their partner to use later, and identify what they thought they did well and what they need to do to improve for the next lesson.

SESSIONS 8 AND 9

Balance – related to apparatus

Consolidation from previous session: to combine a variety of balances showing a range of body shapes (including tucked, narrow, stretched and wide).

LEARNING OBJECTIVES

(The objectives of the session need to be made explicit to the children. They also need to assess the extent to which they have achieved them.)

Physical

1   To be able to balance on the apparatus in a variety of ways.

2   To know what is meant by distributing weight.

Well-being

3   To be able to identify how the body feels after being active and why this is beneficial.

Broader learning

4   To be able to name particular muscle groups.

ASSESSMENT CRITERIA – QUESTIONS TO CONSIDER

1   Can the children use the apparatus to balance in a variety of ways?

2   Can the children transfer their weight from one body part to another?

3   Are they able to describe how they feel after activity?

4   Are they able to name one or two muscle groups in the arms, for example triceps and biceps?

Warm-up

	Content	Teaching points
1	Run in and out of each other (add change of direction, levels and speed) and on the sound of the tambour hold a narrow stretched shape.	Verbalise responses and select one or two children to demonstrate in order to share ideas.
2	Select from skipping, hopping, jumping and running, adding changes of direction, levels and speed. On the sound of the tambour balance in a tucked shape, stretch and tuck again.	Verbalise responses and select one or two children to demonstrate in order to share ideas. Look for smooth transitions between motion and stillness.

3	Repeat the task above but now select three balances from: tucked, narrow, stretched and wide.	You may want to do this several times to give the children the opportunity to share ideas and consolidate skills. Articulate exactly how the children are answering the task.
	DEVELOPING SUPPLENESS – On all fours, alternately arch and round your back (happy cat/angry cat) – for back mobility. Straddle sit and press your tummy down to the floor (easy pressure). **QUESTIONS** – Can the children remember any muscle groups? Remind them of the hamstring, quadriceps and calf, and introduce them to the triceps and biceps.	

Floor work

	Content	Teaching points
1	Practise balancing in different ways using your apparatus. Think about how you use the apparatus to help you balance.	This is an exploratory task – verbalise responses to help share ideas. Remind them about holding/gripping parts of the apparatus and stretching away, leaning against, balancing on, and pulling away from it.
2	Some of you try out different balances on the floor; others try out balances on the apparatus. Now change over.	Encourage all the ideas from previous sessions, i.e. different body parts – different body shapes. Encourage conscious thinking about how to use the apparatus to develop the range of possibilities as noted in the task above.
3	Try to find new balances where you are partly on the floor and partly on, or against, the apparatus.	Verbalise and select two or three children to demonstrate. Highlight strong body tension and good flexibility.
4	Share your balances with a partner.	Verbalise balance on different body parts, the range of body shapes and the uses of the apparatus.
5	Plan, practise and refine a sequence of four balances that you can perform together, using both the floor and apparatus.	Select children to demonstrate balances that are on the apparatus, partly on, and against, using different ways of achieving the balances.
6	In pairs show another pair your sequence.	Children are to feed back against criteria: different body parts, variety of body shapes, use of the apparatus.

Consider these four possibilities when linking balance with apparatus:

- balancing wholly on a piece of apparatus;
- balancing, touching more than one piece of apparatus;
- balancing, touching floor and apparatus (especially getting the children to grip the apparatus where appropriate to develop more ideas);
- balancing away from the apparatus.

Final activity

Leaning against benches or a wall frame, bend and straighten your arms ten times (stronger children will be able to do this arm-strengthening exercise on benches – the less strong, higher up the wall). Which arm muscles are you using?

Stretch up high, reaching up to the ceiling with your fingertips and standing on tiptoes. Gradually roll down your body towards the floor into a tight ball.

Classroom

Children should make a note of their sequence with their partner to use later, and identify what they thought they did well and what they need to do to improve for the next lesson.

Travelling – on large parts (emphasis on sliding)

Consolidation from previous session: to perform balances wholly on the apparatus, touching more than one piece of apparatus, touching the floor and apparatus, and balancing away from the apparatus.

LEARNING OBJECTIVES

(The objectives of the session need to be made explicit to the children. They also need to assess the extent to which they have achieved them.)

Physical

1   To know how to perform sliding actions using the body to push and pull.

2   To replicate a sequence that includes a range of balances with sliding actions.

Well-being

3   To identify what is good in a peer's performance and be able to communicate this in a positive manner.

Broader learning

4   To revise naming particular muscle groups (in arms and/or legs).

ASSESSMENT CRITERIA – QUESTIONS TO CONSIDER

1   Can the children perform a sliding action by pushing and/or pulling?

2   Can they replicate a sequence that includes different balances and sliding actions?

3   Can the children observe each other and give positive, supportive feedback?

4   Are they able to remember one or two muscle groups, for example biceps, triceps, hamstring, quadriceps and calf?

Warm-up

	Content	Teaching points
I	Run in and out of each other (add changes of direction, levels and speed) and on the sound of the tambour hold a two-point balance (two body parts touching the floor).	Highlight strong body tension and extended fingers and toes etc.

| 2 | Select from skipping, hopping, jumping and running (add changes of direction, levels and speed) and on the sound of the tambour hold three-point, one-point, four-point and two-point balances (select one at a time). | Verbalise responses and select one or two children to show. Encourage children to try out each others' ideas. |
| 3 | Select from skipping, hopping, jumping and running (adding changes of direction, levels and speed) and on the sound of the tambour perform three balances on different points, one after the other. | Verbalise responses and emphasise the good technique. |

DEVELOPING SUPPLENESS – Standing, stretch alternate arms upwards – which arm muscles are we stretching? Standing, kick a hand held at shoulder height in various directions (shoulder and hip mobility respectively).

Floor work

	Content	Teaching points
1	Choose a starting position close to the floor. Travel across the floor using rolling, sliding or rocking movements.	Articulate the various responses. Select children to show, and encourage children to try out others' ideas.
2	Repeat, ensuring that all three different actions are included.	Stop and discuss the differences between the actions.
3	Sliding: find different parts of the body you can slide on. Is it possible to slide on these using *pushing* movements and *pulling* movements?	Parts not touching the floor must be extended and held with control during the action. Select examples and highlight this.
4	Stretch out on your side; use your arms to push you into sliding, and then to pull you into sliding.	As above – really stretch your legs off the floor.
5	Try this on your bottom with your legs high in the air. Try it on your tummy with the rest of the body fully stretched.	Tight muscle control in stomach and legs.
6	In pairs plan, perform and refine a sequence that includes two balances and two sliding actions.	Encourage controlled body actions, smooth transitions and bodies to be clearly extended. Select good examples to show and highlight this.
7	In pairs show another pair your sequence.	Pairs are to feed back against given criteria – encourage the children to say what they like and identify whether they are pushing or pulling in their sliding phase; and is the body being held with strong tension?

Apparatus

	Content	Teaching points
1	With your partner perform your sequence using both the floor and apparatus. You may need to adapt some of your movements to achieve this – as practised in the previous sessions.	Encourage children to perform actions wholly on the apparatus, touching more than one piece of apparatus, touching the floor and apparatus, and away from the apparatus. Verbalise responses and show good examples. Check how they are using the apparatus to sustain the balance.
2	Pairs are to watch one another and peer-assess, giving positive feedback and using the given criteria (as detailed above).	Give children the opportunity to incorporate the feedback received into their sequences. This takes time, so practise several times.

Final activity

Lying prone, get up slowly, unfolding your body into an upright position and keeping your feet in one spot. (Ask the children which muscles are being developed in this activity?)
Then stretch up high and hold the stretch.

Classroom

Children should make a note of their sequence with their partner to use later, and identify what they thought they did well and what they need to do to improve for the next lesson.

SESSIONS 12 AND 13

Travelling – on large parts (emphasis on rolling)

Consolidation from previous session: to incorporate balances and sliding actions using the body to push and pull.

LEARNING OBJECTIVES

(The objectives of the session need to be made explicit to the children. They also need to assess the extent to which they have achieved them.)

Physical

1   To know how to perform a variety of rolls.

2   To adapt a sequence from the floor to the apparatus.

Well-being

3   To know that being strong and supple are vital attributes for effective gymnastic performances.

Broader learning

4   To negotiate and collaborate in order to devise a sequence of movements.

ASSESSMENT CRITERIA – QUESTIONS TO CONSIDER

1   Can the children perform the following rolls: log, one leg leading, teddy bear, sideways shoulder, and tuck and stretch?

2   Can they adapt their sequence from the floor to the apparatus?

3   Can the children name the key physical attributes that they need to develop in order to perform effectively in gymnastics?

4   Are they able to share ideas, show their movements to one another and negotiate which movements to select to form a sequence?

Warm-up

	Content	Teaching points
1	Select from skipping, hopping, jumping and running (adding changes of direction and levels) and on the sound of the tambour hold three-point, one-point and four-point balances (select one at a time).	Verbalise responses and highlight strong body tension and extended fingers and toes etc.

2	Slide on various body parts around the room (adding changes of direction). On the sound of the tambour change the action from a pulling to a pushing action and vice versa.	Tight muscle control in stomach and legs – reiterate the need for pushing and pulling.
3	Select from skipping, hopping, jumping and running (adding changes of direction and levels). On the sound of the tambour perform two balances on different numbers of points (body parts) followed by two sliding actions.	Encourage controlled body actions, smooth transitions and bodies to be clearly extended.

DEVELOPING SUPPLENESS – On all fours, lift one leg and try to touch the back of your head with your foot, then tuck the leg under and try to touch your knee to your forehead. Change legs and repeat five times.

QUESTION – In order to be able to perform well in gymnastics our bodies need to be _____ and _____ – what should be in the gaps?

Floor work

(See 'Specific skills guide' – Simple variations in rolling, page 227.)

Children are to work in pairs, with one trying the roll and the other peer-assessing against criteria highlighted by the teacher and then changing over. Mats are not always needed for these rolls, but are when intensively practising, as in this case.

	Content	Teaching points
1	Roll across the mat in a **log** position.	Model or select a child who can give a good demonstration where you can highlight feet together, toes and fingers fully extended and weight taken on the hips.

2	Do as above but with **one leg leading**.	As above, but highlight that the high leg moves across the body to start the movement.
3	Roll across the mat doing the **teddy bear roll**.	Usually there is a child who will be able to model this action. Straddle sit – leg extension and body tension. Take hold of the lower legs/ankles. Lower the body to the side so the shoulder/side of the body is on the floor. Roll across the back and sit up facing the opposite direction. Keep the legs in the astride position throughout the roll.
4	Practise the **sideways shoulder roll**.	Highlight the starting position. Drop the leading shoulder to start the movement, and roll across the shoulders keeping the knees bent. Keep the momentum going and roll over to replicate the starting position.
5	Practise the **tuck and stretch roll**.	Tuck and stretch alternately.
6	With your partner plan, perform and refine a sequence that includes four rolls.	Encourage controlled rolls, smooth transitions and bodies to be clearly extended. Select good examples to show and highlight these criteria.
7	In pairs show another pair your sequence.	Pairs are to feed back against given criteria.

Apparatus

	Content	Teaching points
1	With your partner perform your sequence using both the floor and apparatus. You may need to adapt some of your movements to achieve this.	Encourage children to perform actions wholly on the apparatus, touching more than one piece of apparatus, touching the floor and apparatus, and away from the apparatus. Verbalise responses and show good examples.
2	Pairs are to watch one another and peer-assess, giving positive feedback and using the given criteria (as detailed above).	Give children the opportunity to incorporate the feedback received into their sequences.

Final activity

On all fours, alternately arch and round your back (happy cat/angry cat – back mobility). Sit with good poise – stretch your arms upwards, hold, and then relax.

Classroom

Children should make a note of their sequence with their partner to use later, and identify what they thought they did well and what they need to do to improve for the next lesson.

Travelling – introducing forward roll

(See 'Specific skills guide' – Forward roll, page 218.)

Consolidation from previous session: to consolidate the following rolls: log roll, one leg leading, teddy bear, sideways shoulder, tuck and stretch.

LEARNING OBJECTIVES

(The objectives of the session need to be made explicit to the children. They also need to assess the extent to which they have achieved them.)

Physical

1   To learn how to perform a correct and safe forward roll.

2   To use criteria to improve performance.

Well-being

3   To know that being strong and supple are vital attributes for effective gymnastic performances.

Broader learning

4   To identify muscle groups that are important in activity.

ASSESSMENT CRITERIA – QUESTIONS TO CONSIDER

1   Can the children begin to perform a correct and safe forward roll?

2   Are they able to assess their work against criteria, making adjustments that show improvement?

3   Can the children name the key attributes that they need to develop in order to perform effectively in gymnastics?

4   Are they able to name one or two muscle groups discussed in earlier sessions?

Warm-up

	Content	Teaching points
1	Select from skipping, hopping, jumping and running (adding changes of direction and levels). On the sound of the tambour children remember a roll from the previous session (mats are not needed for this activity).	Verbalise responses and encourage controlled rolls and bodies to be clearly extended. Select one or two children to show and highlight good body tension etc.
2	Repeat and on the sound of the tambour perform two rolls that you have just seen, or select your own.	Verbalise responses and encourage controlled rolls, bodies to be clearly extended and smooth transitions.

3	Repeat and on sound of tambour children select two different rolls.	Verbalise responses and encourage controlled rolls, bodies to be clearly extended and smooth transitions.
	DEVELOPING SUPPLENESS – On all fours, alternately arch and hunch your back (happy cat/angry cat). **DEVELOPING STRENGTH** – Do four squat jumps finishing in a tucked position. Stand with one foot in front of the other, shoulder width apart, and bend the knee of the front leg and stretch the other leg behind for a count of 20, then change over legs. **QUESTIONS** – What muscle groups are working? What are we developing by these stretches and why is that particularly important to gymnastics?		

Floor work

Use mats (ideally two children to a mat, working in pairs). (See 'Specific skills guide' – Forward roll, page 218.)

	Content	Teaching points
1	Rock backwards on to your back and forwards into a sitting position.	Heels to be close to the bottom and chin to chest.
2	Repeat 1, but now come to a standing position as the feet touch down.	Arms reach forward. It may be helpful to reach for a partner's hands to encourage this action.
3	Stand feet astride, hands on the floor in front of the feet, shoulder width apart. Tuck chin to chest and lower the top of the shoulders to the floor and tip over.	Children should take their weight on their hands and transfer carefully on to the shoulders. Try to encourage stretched legs during the roll, tucked as standing phase begins. This should be a controlled action.
4	Those who master 3 begin the roll from a squat position. Those who are not ready continue with 3.	Initial movement therefore goes *forward*. For some children reaching forward to grasp a partner's hands at the end of the roll is helpful ('Specific skills guide' – page 219, point 2).
5	Free practice, aiming for precision and control of all rolls (i.e. to include those done earlier).	Don't let the children rush at this stage and make sure they try a range of different rolls so they don't get dizzy.
6	With a partner plan, perform and refine a sequence that includes four rolls.	Encourage rolls, smooth transitions, strong body tension and extended fingers and toes. Select good examples to highlight these criteria.
7	In pairs show another pair your sequence.	Pairs are to feed back against given criteria. Allow children to use feedback to improve performance.

Apparatus

	Content	Teaching points
1	With your partner perform your sequence using both the floor and apparatus. You may need to adapt some of your movements to achieve this.	Encourage children to perform actions wholly on the apparatus, touching more than one piece of apparatus, touching the floor and apparatus, and away from the apparatus. Verbalise responses and show good examples.
2	Pairs are to watch one another and peer-assess, giving positive feedback and using the given criteria (as detailed above).	Give children the opportunity to address the feedback received and improve their sequences.

Final activity

Repeat the actions for developing strength and suppleness practised earlier in the session.

(It is important that the children know that muscles can be stretched further when they are really warm and that this is often near the end of an activity.)

Classroom

Children should make a note of their sequence with their partner to use later, and identify what they thought they did well and what they need to do to improve for the next lesson.

SESSIONS 16 AND 17

Jumping

(See 'Specific skills guide' – Jumping, page 216.)

Consolidation from previous session: to learn to perform the forward roll.

LEARNING OBJECTIVES

(The objectives of the session need to be made explicit to the children. They also need to assess the extent to which they have achieved them.)

Physical

1   To know how to perform a variety of jumps.

2   To use criteria to improve performance.

Well-being

3   To know some activities that will develop strength and suppleness.

Broader learning

4   To relate knowledge of 'degrees' in performing turning jumps.

ASSESSMENT CRITERIA – QUESTIONS TO CONSIDER

1   Can the children perform the following jumps: straight, star, scissor etc.?

2   Can they assess each other's movements against given criteria and then improve their performances?

3   Are they able to suggest and perform activities that develop strength and suppleness?

4   Can they relate their knowledge of 'degrees' in performing turning jumps?

Warm-up

Position mats around the hall.

	Content	Teaching points
1	Select from skipping, hopping, jumping and running (adding changes of direction, levels and speed, zigzag and curved pathways). On the sound of the tambour remember a roll from the previous session and perform it carefully on a mat.	Verbalise responses and encourage controlled rolls and bodies to be clearly extended. Select one or two children to show and highlight good body tension etc.
2	As above, but on the sound of the tambour perform two rolls that you have just seen, or select your own.	Verbalise responses and encourage controlled rolls, bodies to be clearly extended and smooth transitions.

3	As above, but on the sound of the tambour select two different rolls.	Verbalise responses and encourage controlled rolls, bodies to be clearly extended and smooth transitions.
	DEVELOPING SUPPLENESS AND STRENGTH – In pairs, encourage children to try out ideas for actions that develop both strength and suppleness. Share ideas with the class.	

Floor work

	Content	Teaching points
1	Jump around the room keeping two feet together.	Highlight soft knees on take-off and landing.
2	Perform a jump that is high and extended. Practise and refine.	Bend the knees, swing the arms above the head, keeping the body straight and the head high. Select one or two good examples. Watch each other and feed back against criteria.
3	Perform a 'star jump'. Practise and refine.	Take off with feet together, straddle the legs and arms wide in the air, and bring them together with soft knees for landing. Select one or two good examples. Watch each other and feed back against criteria.
4	Perform a 'scissor jump'. Practise and refine.	Start with feet together, and kick one foot up followed by the other. Keep the head held high. Select one or two good examples. Watch each other and feed back against criteria.
5	With your partner perform a jump with a 45°, 90°, 180° and 360° turn. Practise and refine.	Discuss degrees (°) with children to relate to this task. Use arms and bend knees to give you lift and momentum. Select one or two good examples. Watch each other and feed back against criteria.
6	With your partner plan, perform and refine a sequence that includes the four jumps.	Encourage smooth transitions, strong body tension and extended fingers and toes. Select good examples to highlight these criteria.
7	Select pairs of children to perform their sequences.	Focus children's attention on particular pairs and encourage them to say what they are doing well against the given criteria. Make sure all the children have the opportunity to show.

Apparatus

	Content	Teaching points
1	With your partner perform your sequence using both the floor and apparatus. You may need to adapt some of your movements to achieve this.	Encourage children to perform actions wholly on the apparatus, touching more than one piece of apparatus, touching the floor and apparatus, and away from the apparatus. Verbalise responses and show good examples.
2	Pairs are to watch one another and peer-assess giving positive feedback and using the given criteria (as detailed above).	Give children the opportunity to incorporate the feedback received into their sequences.

Final activity

Lying prone, get up keeping your feet in one spot (arm strength). Stretch up high and very slowly sink to the floor, making your body into a tight ball. Stretch out again.

Classroom

Children should make a note of their sequence with their partner to use later, and identify what they thought they did well and what they need to do to improve for the next lesson.

Jumping, balancing and travelling

Consolidation from previous session: to combine a variety of jumps in a sequence that includes straight, star, scissor and turning jumps performed at 45°, 90°,180° and 360°.

LEARNING OBJECTIVES

(The objectives of the session need to be made explicit to the children. They also need to assess the extent to which they have achieved them.)

Physical

1   To know how to perform a variety of jumps, balances and travelling actions.

2   To know how to link contrasting movements smoothly.

Well-being

3   To be able to suggest warm-up activities.

Broader learning

4   To compare and contrast actions, identifying similarities and differences.

ASSESSMENT CRITERIA – QUESTIONS TO CONSIDER

1   Can the children perform a variety of jumps, balances and travelling actions?

2   Do the children link contrasting actions smoothly?

3   Are the children able to suggest and perform suitable warm-up activities?

4   Are the children able to watch others and identify similarities and differences in another's movements?

Warm-up

Position mats around the hall.

	Content	Teaching points
1	Select from skipping, hopping, jumping and running (adding changes of direction, levels and speed, zigzag and curved pathways) and on the sound of the tambour remember a particular jump from the previous session.	Verbalise responses, encourage controlled jumps and bodies to be clearly extended. Select one or two children to show and highlight soft knees on take-off and landing, good body tension etc.
2	Select from skipping, hopping, jumping and running (adding changes of direction, levels and speed, zigzag and curved pathways) and on the sound of the tambour perform two jumps that you have just seen or select your own.	Verbalise responses and encourage explosive jumps with bodies clearly extended and smooth transitions.

3	In pairs, children decide on a warm-up activity and try it out.	Verbalise children's responses. Question: What makes a warm-up effective? (For example, it raises the heart rate, increases body temperature etc.)
	DEVELOPING SUPPLENESS – Slowly circle straight arms forward in a circular position, brushing the ears. Straddle sit and press your tummy down to the floor (easy pressure). **DEVELOPING STRENGTH** – Perform five squat jumps – stand up straight with your feet together and bring both knees up to the chest. Keep your head upright.	

Floor work

	Content	Teaching points
1	Hold a balance as a starting position and move into another balance. Practise, perform and refine.	Encourage contrasting balances, for example tucked, narrow, wide or stretched balances. Control with good body tension to ensure the transition is smooth. Share one or two good examples.
2	Combine your balances with a sliding action where you 'push' or 'pull'.	Encourage strong body tension, smooth transitions and feet and hands to be fully extended.
3	In pairs, show each other your sequences.	Children are to watch each other and identify similarities and differences in each other's movements. Encourage discussion.
4	Work on a sequence with your partner that includes some of each other's actions and includes contrast in body shapes.	Verbalise responses and select one or two groups to demonstrate highlighting smooth transitions, questioning the children on how this was achieved.
5	Add a roll and a jump.	Encourage children to put the actions in a different order to make it more pleasing to an audience. Remember jumps learned previously.
6	Explore, perform and refine your sequence.	Encourage smooth transitions, strong body tension and extended fingers and toes. Select good examples to highlight these criteria.
7	Select pairs of children to perform their sequences for the rest of the class.	Focus children's attention on individual pairs and encourage them to say what they are doing well against the given criteria. Make sure all the children have the opportunity to show.

Apparatus

	Content	Teaching points
1	With your partner perform your sequence using both the floor and apparatus. You may need to adapt some of your movements to achieve this.	Encourage children to perform actions wholly on the apparatus, touching more than one piece of apparatus, touching the floor and apparatus, and away from the apparatus. Verbalise responses and show good examples.
2	Pairs are to watch one another and peer-assess giving positive feedback and using the given criteria (as detailed above).	Give children the opportunity to incorporate the feedback received into their sequences.

Final activity

Slowly stretch the body into the air and, as you uncurl, 'explode' into a jump. Then slowly curl the body tightly. Uncurl and stand up straight.

Classroom

Children should make a note of their sequence with their partner to use later, and identify what they thought they did well and what they need to do to improve for the next lesson.

Assessment activity

This session will assess children's knowledge and understanding gained from the sessions throughout the year. Children should be encouraged to take responsibility for their own learning by identifying what they can achieve, what they need to do to develop and how they will do this.

LEARNING OBJECTIVES

(The objectives of the session need to be made explicit to the children. They also need to assess the extent to which they have achieved them.)

Physical

1   To perform a sequence of contrasting actions.

2   To adapt a sequence performed on the floor to include both the floor and apparatus.

3   To remember and perform the sequence with consistency, coordination and control.

Well-being

4   To know that strength and suppleness are key attributes of a gymnast.

Broader learning

5   To identify actions and movements that they can perform well, and know one or two ways in which to improve.

DISCUSSION

Discuss and share ideas of the key attributes of a gymnast and why being strong and supple is important.

Talk about what constitutes good work and how improvements can be made.

ASSESSMENT CRITERIA – QUESTIONS TO CONSIDER

1   Can the children perform contrasting actions in a sequence?

2   Can they adapt their sequence from the floor to include both the floor and apparatus?

3   Can they remember and perform the sequence with consistency, coordination and control?

4   Can the children talk about what a gymnast needs to develop physically and so improve their performance?

5   Can they identify actions and movements that they can perform well, and know one or two ways in which they can improve?

OUTCOME

Some children will achieve, some will excel and some will achieve less.

Warm-up

	Content	Teaching points
1	Play the Bean Game – children move around the hall according to the bean that is called out: runner bean – running; jumping bean – jumping; chilli bean – rubbing all body parts to keep warm; jelly bean – wobbling like jelly; frozen bean – being still; baked bean – lying down as if looking at the sky; butter bean – sliding on your bottom.	Verbalise the children's body actions and highlight where they are demonstrating with good control and tension.

Floor work

	Content	Teaching points
1	With a partner devise a sequence that includes one or more of each of the following: balances, sliding actions, rolls and jumps.	Encourage balances on different parts of the body (small and large) and different body shapes (tucked, narrow, stretched and wide etc.). Sliding actions are to include push and/or pull. Rolls: one leg leading, teddy bear, sideways shoulder, tuck and stretch etc. Jumps: straight, star, scissor and various turns.
2	Practise and refine, and when you can remember your sequence add a contrasting action to it.	Circulate and set differentiated challenges to accommodate individual abilities. Show one or two examples and highlight good body tension and control, smooth transitions etc.
3	Practise and refine, and when you can remember your sequence, add a further contrasting action.	Encourage children to have five different movements (although this will be dependent on ability). Ask children what they can do well and what they need to do to improve.
4	Consider how you are going to start and finish your sequence. There should be clear beginnings and endings that are held still for a short period of time.	Select some children to show and highlight contrasting actions with pleasing starting and finishing positions.
5	In pairs name yourselves 1 and 2 – 2s are to show 1s their sequence and then change over.	Encourage children to identify contrasting actions with pleasing starting and finishing positions. The children should now discuss what they did well and what they need to do to improve.

Apparatus

	Content	Teaching points
1	In your pairs, adapt your sequences using the floor and apparatus.	Highlight where children are wholly using the apparatus, touching more than one piece of apparatus, and touching the floor and apparatus.
2	One pair is to watch another and identify good body tension, extensions, smooth transitions and contrasting actions.	Can they discuss with one another what they did well and what they want to do to improve?
	ASSESSMENT – By the teacher (in conjunction with a teaching assistant where applicable), and also peer-assessment by the children. Use ICT to record as many performances as possible so the children can self-assess during the lesson and in the classroom. This can also be kept as a record of their achievement.	

Final activity

Walk around the room, stretch up high and curl up tightly. Wait to be tapped to line up (enrol some children to help).

Classroom

Children should make a note of their sequence with their partner for their records. They may use these in the next academic year.

The sessions

Year 4

SESSION 1
Assessment activity

This first session is for an initial assessment of the children's capabilities to ascertain what they know and what they can do.

This session relates, in part, to the final assessment task in Year 3.

LEARNING OBJECTIVES

(The objectives of the session need to be made explicit to the children. They also need to assess the extent to which they have achieved them.)

Physical

1   To perform a sequence of contrasting actions.

2   To adapt a sequence performed on the floor to include both the floor and apparatus.

3   To remember and perform the sequence with consistency, coordination and control.

Well-being

4   To know that strength and suppleness are key attributes of a gymnast.

Broader learning

5   To identify actions and movements that they can perform well, and know one or two ways in which to improve.

DISCUSSION

Discuss and share ideas of the key attributes of a gymnast and why being strong and supple is important.

Talk about what constitutes good work and how improvements can be made.

ASSESSMENT CRITERIA – QUESTIONS TO CONSIDER

1   Can the children perform contrasting actions in a sequence?

2   Can they adapt their sequence from the floor to include both the floor and apparatus?

3   Can they remember and perform the sequence with consistency, coordination and control?

4   Can the children talk about what a gymnast needs to develop physically and so improve their performance?

5   Are they able to identify actions and movements that they can perform well, and know one or two ways in which they can improve?

OUTCOME

Some children will achieve, some will excel and some will achieve less.

Warm-up

	Content	Teaching points
1	Play the Bean Game – children move around the hall according to the bean that is called out: runner bean – running; jumping bean – jumping; chilli bean – rubbing all body parts to keep warm; jelly bean – wobbling like jelly; frozen bean – being still; baked bean – lying down as if looking at the sky; butter bean – sliding on your bottom.	Verbalise the children's body actions and highlight where they are demonstrating with good control and tension.

Floor work

	Content	Teaching points
1	With a partner devise a sequence that includes one or more of the following: balances, sliding actions, rolls and jumps.	Encourage balances on different parts of the body (small and large) and different body shapes (tucked, narrow, stretched and wide etc.). Sliding actions are to include push and/or pull. Rolls: one leg leading, teddy bear, sideways shoulder, tuck and stretch etc. Jumps: straight, star, scissor and various turns.
2	Practise and refine, and when you can remember your sequence add a contrasting action to it.	Circulate and set differentiated challenges to accommodate individual abilities. Show one or two examples and highlight good body tension and control, smooth transitions etc.
3	Practise and refine, and when you can remember your sequence, add a further contrasting action.	Encourage children to have five different movements (although this will be dependent on ability). Ask children what they can do well and what they need to do to improve.
4	Consider how you are going to start and finish your sequence. There should be clear beginnings and endings that are held still for a short period of time.	Select some children to show and highlight contrasting actions with pleasing starting and finishing positions.
5	In pairs name yourselves 1 and 2 – 2s are to show 1s their sequence and then change over.	Encourage children to identify contrasting actions with pleasing starting and finishing positions. The children should now discuss what they did well and what they need to do to improve.

Apparatus

1	In your pairs adapt your sequences using the floor and apparatus.	Highlight where children are wholly using the apparatus, touching more than one piece of apparatus, touching the floor and apparatus.
2	One pair is to watch another and identify good body tension, extensions, smooth transitions and contrasting actions.	Can they discuss with one another what they did well and what they want to improve?
	ASSESSMENT – By the teacher (in conjunction with a teaching assistant where applicable), and also peer-assessment by the children. Use ICT to record as many performances as possible so that the children can self-assess during the lesson and in the classroom. This can also be kept as a record of their achievement.	

Final activity

Walk around the room, stretch up high and curl up tightly. Wait to be tapped to line up (enrol some children to help).

Classroom

Children should make a note of their sequence with their partner to use later, and identify what they thought they did well and what they need to do to improve for the next lesson.

(a)

Balancing: (a) on a large body part, (b) on small body parts and (c) with a partner.

(b)

(c)

Travelling – jumping and rolling

Consolidation from previous session: this session directs the children's attention quite specifically towards improving the skill of jumping and rolling in a variety of ways, allowing them to consolidate previously learned skills and develop new ones.

LEARNING OBJECTIVES

(The objectives of the session need to be made explicit to the children. They also need to assess the extent to which they have achieved them.)

Physical

1   To continue to develop performance in a variety of jumps and rolls.

2   To use criteria to improve their and others' performances.

Well-being

3   To articulate the kinds of activity that will develop their strength and suppleness.

Broader learning

4   To be able to plan the timing of actions with their partners.

ASSESSMENT CRITERIA – QUESTIONS TO CONSIDER

1   Can the children perform a variety of jumps and rolls with control and coordination?

2   Can the children assess their own and others' performances against given criteria?

3   Can they suggest and perform activities that develop their strength and suppleness?

4   Within a sequence, are the children able to perform actions in unison?

Warm-up

See Year 3, sessions 12 and 13 for details of rolling, and also the 'Specific skills guide' – Rolling (page 227).

	Content	Teaching points
1	Run in and out of each other (adding changes of direction, speed, levels and pathways) and on the sound of the tambour perform a pike jump and log roll.	Pike – highlight soft knees on take-off and landing, extended arms, pointed fingers etc. Bend the knees, swing the arms above the head, keep the body straight and the head high. Log – extend your body fully, with arms above the head, stretched out with fingers and toes pointed, and roll using the hips. Select one or two good examples and highlight key criteria.

2	Run in and out of each other (adding changes of direction, speed, levels and pathways) and on the sound of the tambour perform a star jump and teddy bear roll.	Star – take off with your feet together, straddle the legs and arms wide in the air, and bring them together with soft knees for landing. Teddy bear roll – when rolling to the right, pull your right leg across and over. Roll on the shoulder and look at your feet. Select one or two good examples and highlight key criteria.
3	Run in and out of each other (adding changes of direction, speed, levels and pathways) and on the sound of the tambour perform a scissor jump and a sideways shoulder roll.	Scissor – start with your feet together, then kick one foot up followed by the other. Hold the head high. Sideways shoulder roll – start as shown in the diagram (page 228), drop your leading shoulder, roll on your back to the other shoulder and push up with your leg so you complete as shown. Select one or two good examples and highlight key criteria.
4	Run in and out of each other (adding changes of direction, speed, levels and pathways) and on the sound of the tambour select a jump and a roll of your choice.	Select one or two good examples and highlight key criteria.
	DEVELOPING SUPPLENESS AND STRENGTH – In pairs, encourage children to try out ideas of actions that develop both suppleness and strength. Share good examples with the whole class and then have all the children perform them.	

Floor work

	Content	Teaching points
1	In pairs, practise a tuck jump. Observe each other and give feedback against given criteria.	Start with both feet together. Jump your legs up towards your arms (don't bring the upper body down to meet the legs). Keep the body upright.
2	In pairs, practise jumping from one foot to another with a turn. Observe each other and give feedback against given criteria.	Balance on one leg, use the arms to lift and turn you around so that you land on the other leg facing in the opposite direction.
3	With your partner plan a sequence that includes two jumps and two rolls. Make sure that one of the jumps is performed in unison. Practise and refine.	Work out the sequence and which jump you are going to do at the same time. Count out loud to help you with the timing. Select one or two good examples as models.

4	Try changing the order of your sequence to make it more pleasing to an audience. You could reverse it.	Verbalise responses and select pairs to show.
5	In pairs, show another pair your sequence.	Children are to watch each other and feed back on whether the jump is performed in unison during the sequence.

Apparatus

	Content	Teaching points
1	In pairs, plan, perform and adapt your sequence using both the floor and apparatus. Add clear and interesting starting and finishing positions.	Do you need to change order? As well as jumping on and off, can you also move through, around, along, partly on, partly off etc.? Verbalise responses and select one or two creative examples to show.
2	One pair is to watch another and give constructive feedback.	Assess against whether they have a variety of jumps, perform in unison and at different times, and have good body tension and control.

Final activity

In twos, try to turn your partner over (partner resists) – feel the tension throughout the body.

Sit with good body poise.

Classroom

Children should make a note of their sequence with their partner to use later, and identify what they thought they did well and what they need to do to improve for the next lesson.

Travelling – jumping and rolling

Consolidation from previous session: in pairs, to perform a variety of jumping and rolling actions in a sequence, with one jump being performed in unison. Adapt the sequence on to both floor and apparatus.

LEARNING OBJECTIVES

(The objectives of the session need to be made explicit to the children. They also need to assess the extent to which they have achieved them.)

Physical

1   To learn how to perform a correct and safe backward roll.

2   To use criteria to improve performance.

Well-being

3   To be able to communicate ideas to another.

Broader learning

4   To be able to explore a range of ideas.

ASSESSMENT CRITERIA – QUESTIONS TO CONSIDER

1   Can the children perform a correct and safe backward roll?

2   Are they able to assess their and others' work against criteria, making adjustments to show improvement?

3   Can the children communicate effectively and share ideas to achieve an ultimate performance?

4   Are the children willing to try a variety of body shapes to develop their work?

Warm-up

	Content	Teaching points
1	Run in and out of each other (adding changes of direction, speed, levels and pathways) and on the sound of the tambour perform a tuck jump.	Start with both feet together. Jump your legs up towards your arms (don't bring the upper body down to meet the legs). Keep your body upright.
2	Run in and out of each other (adding changes of direction, speed, levels and pathways) and on the sound of the tambour jump from one foot to the other with a turn.	Balance on one leg, using your arms to lift and turn you around so that you land on the other leg facing in the opposite direction.

3	Run in and out of each other (adding changes of direction, speed, levels and pathways) and on the sound of the tambour select a jump of your own.	Select one or two good examples and highlight key criteria.
4	Run in and out of each other (adding changes of direction, speed, levels and pathways) and on the sound of the tambour all jump at the same time, in unison.	Reinforce that unison means 'together'.
	DEVELOPING SUPPLENESS – Caterpillar walk – fix your hands on the floor and gradually bring your straight legs closer to your hands, then walk the hands away from the feet. **DEVELOPING STRENGTH** – Bounce on the spot, gradually increasing the height.	

Floor work

Use all the mats; children should be in groups.

	Content	Teaching points
1	Revise the forward roll.	See Year 3, sessions 14 and 15, and the 'Specific skills guide' – Rolling (page 227).
	The teacher will then demonstrate the technique of the backward roll (using an able child) to the whole class. After this he/she will work with one group at a time teaching the backward roll. (See 'Specific skills guide' – Backward roll, page 220.) The rest of the class will work as directed on task 2 below.	
2	With your partner on your mat make up a pattern of three rolls that cross the mat and sometimes change direction. Let the final roll bring you to your feet and finish with a jump (controlled landing).	Ensure preparation for the next roll at the end of the previous roll. Encourage peer-assessment.
3	In pairs, show another pair your sequence.	Children are to watch each other and feed back on whether the rolls show changes in direction and the transition between movements is smooth.

Apparatus

Children are to put the apparatus out as shown in the section, 'Apparatus diagrams and task cards' (page 229). Task cards should be used for this work.

Children should be discouraged from hurrying through these activities. The aim is for quality and skill, so control and concentration are essential. Give children time to practise each task and rotate after sufficient practice and refinement time.

	Content	Teaching points
1	Group 1 – Find ways to combine rolls and jumps using the floor and apparatus. Make sure you include a turn when you jump.	Again, emphasise correct arm action and correct movement of the head and shoulders and a controlled landing.
2	Group 2 – Travel up the plank gripping it with the hands, jumping the feet from one side to the other. Explore a range of jumps and rolls when you dismount.	Emphasise a strong push from the legs and working hard on the arms. Encourage peer-assessment.
3	Take a short approach run to the bench, take off from one foot to land on two feet on the bench. Then jump off to land on the mat. Vary the shape of the jump in the air.	Try to encourage the 'hurdle' step approach. Again, encourage tension in the body to hold a clear shape in the air (see 'Specific skills guide' – Jumping, page 216). Encourage peer-assessment.
4	Practise forward and backward rolls, trying to vary the shape of the legs during the roll.	Combine legs together, apart, bent, straight. Note hand placement for the straddle roll (see 'Specific skills guide' – Rolling, page 227).
5	Squat jump on to the box. Spring off showing a clear stretched body shape in the air before landing.	A strong push from the legs is essential for a squat jump. Children can squat up on their knees if they have difficulty getting their feet through on to the box.
6	Practise a straddle forward roll carefully down the slope.	*The teacher should stay at this station.* Feet are placed either side of the benches when finishing the roll (see 'Specific skills guide' – Rolling, page 227).

Final activity

In the same groups, practise follow my leader squat jumping around the mat – mats need to be pulled away from the benches. Put the apparatus away. Stand well.

Classroom

Children should make a note of their floor work sequence with their partner to use later, and identify what they thought they did well and what they need to do to improve for the next lesson.

Balance – with travelling into and out of balance – and introducing the headstand

(See 'Specific skills guide' – Headstand, page 221.)

Consolidation from previous session: to revise and continue to learn forward and backward rolls.

LEARNING OBJECTIVES

(The objectives of the session need to be made explicit to the children. They also need to assess the extent to which they have achieved them.)

Physical

1   To learn to perform a correct and safe headstand.

2   To understand the terms mirror, match, canon and unison when working with a partner.

Well-being

3   To add to the range of activities that will develop strength and suppleness.

Broader learning

4   To know what a ¼, ½, ¾ and whole turn are in degrees.

ASSESSMENT CRITERIA – QUESTIONS TO CONSIDER

1   Can the children perform a correct and safe headstand?

2   Are they able to work with a partner, showing mirroring, matching and working in canon or unison – and can they identify the different actions?

3   Can they suggest and perform activities that develop their strength and suppleness?

4   Are they able to perform a ¼, ½, ¾ and whole turn and do they know the equivalent in degrees?

Warm-up

	Content	Teaching points
1	Run in and out of each other (adding changes of direction, speed, levels and pathways) and on the sound of the tambour jump with a ¼ turn.	Emphasise lifting the arms and turning the shoulder and head, and a controlled landing. What is a ¼ turn in degrees?

2	Run in and out of each other (adding changes of direction, speed, levels and pathways) and on the sound of the tambour jump with a ½ turn.	Verbalise responses and select one or two children to demonstrate good technique. What is a ½ turn in degrees?
3	Run in and out of each other (adding changes of direction, speed, levels and pathways) and on the sound of the tambour jump with a ¾ turn.	Verbalise responses and select one or two children to demonstrate good technique. What is a ¾ turn in degrees?
4	Run in and out of each other (adding changes of direction, speed, levels and pathways) and on the sound of the tambour, taking care, jump turning 360°.	This is difficult to perform with control. Emphasise lifting the arms and turning the shoulder and head, and a controlled landing. Select children with good technique and encourage them to explain their technique.
	DEVELOPING SUPPLENESS AND STRENGTH – In pairs, encourage children to try out ideas of actions that develop both suppleness and strength. Share good examples with the whole class and then ask all the children perform them.	

Floor work

Use all the mats.

	Content	Teaching points
1	Show a range of different balances using different parts of the body.	Children should use small parts, large parts, combinations etc.
2	Repeat stretching further and holding clear body shapes.	Revise the feeling of what is balance – a feeling of being 'perched'.
3	All hold a shoulder balance. Use a roll to bring you out of the balance and on to your feet.	Point out the different directions the roll can take. The body must prepare itself for the roll so it is ready to transfer to the feet. Repeat several times. Peer-assess.
4	With a partner, find a balance and practise ways of rolling out of it.	Verbalise responses. Remind them of forward and backward rolls and different ways of performing – for example, combining legs together, apart, bent or straight.
5	Can you find other ways of getting out of the balance?	Discuss other ways of travelling apart from rolling (jumping, sliding, rocking, spinning etc.).
6	With a partner, devise a sequence where you move into and out of a balance. Think about how you are working together. For example, are your actions mirrored or matched, or are you working in canon or unison?	Select examples that explain the terms mirrored, matched, canon and unison. Remind children of the different jumps and rolls they have performed in previous lessons.

| 7 | In pairs, show another pair your sequence. | Children are to watch each other and feed back on where sequences show examples of actions being mirrored, matched, in canon or in unison. |

Apparatus

Children are to put out the apparatus in fours and (depending on class size) should work in pairs, two to each station. Encourage children to peer-support and share the space. They should take turns when they want to go through their whole sequence using the floor and apparatus.

The teacher will then demonstrate the technique of the headstand (using an able child) to the whole class. After this he/she will work with one group at a time teaching the headstand.

The rest of the class will work as directed on task 2 below.

	Content	Teaching points
1	Select a group at a time – teach the headstand.	See 'Specific skills guide' – Headstand (page 221).
2	Using the apparatus, adapt your paired floor work sequence on to both the floor and apparatus.	Remind children of how they can wholly use the apparatus, touch more than one piece of apparatus, or touch the floor and apparatus. And can they vary the ways they perform, for example mirroring, matching or working in canon or unison? Encourage peer-assessment.

Final activity

Lie face down. Raise your head and chest, clap five times and lower your head and chest. Repeat (this is a back-strengthening activity). Stretch out fully and hold the stretch. Slowly stand.

Classroom

Children should make a note of their sequence with their partner to use later, and identify what they thought they did well and what they need to do to improve for the next lesson.

Travelling – achieving variety using body shape and speed emphasis

Consolidation from previous session: travelling into and out of balance using rolls and jumps learned in previous sessions – and performing a headstand.

LEARNING OBJECTIVES

(The objectives of the session need to be made explicit to the children. They also need to assess the extent to which they have achieved them.)

Physical

1   To learn to perform a movement varying the body shape and assess what might occur.

2   To understand that some movements have natural fast speeds and others slow.

Well-being

3   To articulate the changes that happen to the body during activity, and the benefits to health and well-being of being active.

Broader learning

4   To remember and name muscle groups.

ASSESSMENT CRITERIA – QUESTIONS TO CONSIDER

1   Can the children perform the same movement with various body shapes and then assess what might occur, for example a tucked, extended, feet apart/together roll etc.?

2   Can they recognise that a jump is a naturally fast action, whereas a balance is more pleasing for an audience when performed in a controlled slow manner?

3   Can the children talk about the changes that happen to their bodies when they are active and identify some benefits to their health and well-being?

4   Are they able to remember and name muscle groups?

Warm-up

	Content	Teaching points
1	Run in and out of each other (adding changes of direction, speed, levels and pathways) and on the sound of the tambour hold a balance on a small body part.	Verbalise responses. Expect controlled movement into the balance.

2	Run in and out of each other (adding changes of direction, speed, levels and pathways) and on the sound of the tambour hold a balance on a large body part.	What changes are occurring to your body now that you are becoming more active? How is this beneficial to health and well-being? Share ideas.
3	Run in and out of each other (adding changes of direction, speed, levels and pathways) and on the sound of the tambour move from one balance to another.	Name the muscle groups that are being used in the actions.
4	Run in and out of each other (adding changes of direction, speed, levels and pathways) and on the sound of the tambour move from one balance to another, and finish holding a shoulder balance.	Emphasise the importance of controlled movements and concentration in order to achieve this.
	DEVELOPING SUPPLENESS – On all fours, touch your knees to your forehead and then your foot to the back of your head – repeat three times. Repeat with the other foot. Caterpillar walk – fix your hands to the floor and gradually bring straight legs closer to your hands, then walk your hands away from your feet.	

Floor work

Use all the mats.

	Content	Teaching points
1	Begin on your shoulders, and rock or roll to arrive on your bottom.	Hold with strong body tension and concentrate so movements are controlled. Select one or two good examples to show.
2	Begin similarly and move to arrive on different body part(s).	Emphasise clearly held starting and finishing positions. Verbalise children's ideas.
3	Arrive on your bottom (as in task 1) in tucked or extended position, emphasising one side of hip, legs apart/together etc.	All these are possible variations. Singly or together they may offer many opportunities for variety. Ask the children to discuss them.
4	With a partner, devise a sequence that includes a balance, a jump, a roll and a hands/feet action. Plan, perform and refine.	Children experiment with (a) different kinds of action, and (b) different ways of ordering the actions. Select one or two pairs to demonstrate.

5	Use your action phase (sequence) and see if you can make some parts fast and some slow. Include changes of shape in the actions too. Plan, practise and refine.	It is vital that children identify the natural speed of some actions (for example, jump = fast; arriving at balance = slow). Discuss this and identify those actions where the speed can be changed.
6	Pairs are to show (select several pairs at a time so all the class have the opportunity to show).	Concentrate the children's attention on different pairs, and encourage them to highlight where the change of speed occurs in the performance.

Apparatus

	Content	Teaching points
1	Using the apparatus, adapt your sequence on to both the floor and apparatus.	Remind children of the different jumps, rolls and balances they have performed in previous lessons and how they can wholly use the apparatus, touch more than one piece of apparatus, or touch the floor and apparatus. They can also vary the ways they perform, for example mirroring, matching or working in canon or unison.
2	One pair is to watch another pair and give constructive feedback.	Assess against variety of body shapes and change of speed.

Final activity
In pairs, practise controlled follow my leader squat jumping – change leader. (This is a leg-strengthening activity.) Stand well to finish.

Classroom
Children should make a note of their sequence with their partner to use later, and identify what they thought they did well and what they need to do to improve for the next lesson.

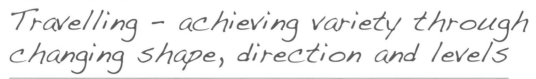

Travelling – achieving variety through changing shape, direction and levels

Consolidation from previous session: performing actions with changes of shape and speed.

LEARNING OBJECTIVES

(The objectives of the session need to be made explicit to the children. They also need to assess the extent to which they have achieved them.)

Physical

1   To learn to perform actions with varied body shapes at different levels and in different directions.

2   To know why it is important to warm up prior to activity and how to do so.

Well-being

3   To revise safety issues concerning the use of space and the possibility of obstructions.

Broader learning

4   To know that a healthy balanced diet is important in maximising sporting achievement.

ASSESSMENT CRITERIA – QUESTIONS TO CONSIDER

1   Can the children perform actions with varied body shapes at different levels and with directional changes?

2   Are they able to lead a partner through a short warm-up and understand why they are doing so?

3   Do the children always move around the hall safely, avoiding their peers and other obstructions?

4   Are they able to name some of the foods that make up a balance diet and know how these provide nourishment for effective activity?

Warm-up

	Content	Teaching points
1	In pairs, one child leads his/her partner through a short warm-up routine.	Make sure that the intensity starts slowly and gradually increases. Try to include some of the previous actions that you have learned.
2	Change over so that the other person leads the warm-up.	Can you think of different movements and actions? What do you need to be aware of when you are travelling around the hall?

3	Discuss as a whole class why warm-ups are needed and share examples of good warm-up activities. Discuss the different foods that provide nourishment for physical activity (for example the benefits of carbohydrates and why).	Select children to demonstrate a warm-up and encourage the whole class to have a go.
	DEVELOPING SUPPLENESS AND STRENGTH – In pairs, encourage children to try out ideas of actions that develop both suppleness and strength. Share good examples with the whole class and then have all the children perform them.	

Floor work

Mats may be useful here but are not essential.

	Content	Teaching points
1	Travel by rolling and jumping, and include a hands/feet action.	Verbalise responses. Select one or two good examples to show.
2	Show your sequence to a partner. Once you have seen both movements, plan a sequence together by negotiating which movements and actions from each other's to include.	Support children in negotiating and encourage them to try out each other's ideas and adapt them if necessary so that they can both perform.
3	Add a balance that becomes a clear starting and finishing position.	Emphasise clearly held starting and finishing positions – full body tension. Verbalise children's ideas.
4	Practise your sequence until you remember it. Now add a change of level and direction to some of the movements where it feels right to do this.	Children experiment (a) with different levels, and (b) by performing movements with changes of direction. Select one or two pairs to demonstrate.
5	Plan, practise, refine and experiment with the order of the movements, and think about how you are working together. For example, are your actions mirrored, matched or are you working in canon or unison?	Select examples that remind children of the terms mirrored, matched, canon and unison.
6	In pairs, show another pair your sequence.	Children are to watch each other and feed back on where sequences show examples of changes in levels and direction.

Apparatus

	Content	Teaching points
1	Using the apparatus, adapt your sequence on to both the floor and apparatus. Make sure that you use the space well by starting away from the apparatus and moving towards it, or begin on the apparatus and travel away from it.	Select one or two pairs of children who are using space well to show. Emphasise the need to show clear changes of level and direction.
2	One pair is to watch another pair and give constructive feedback.	Assess against how well the pair have used levels, direction and space in their sequence. Talking through each other's work often assists children in this, for example 'you began with a roll going forwards, and then you . . .'.

Final activity

Hold a high balance for a count of 5 and slowly move into a low balance for a count of 5, finishing by sitting with good poise.

Classroom

Children should make a note of their sequence with their partner to use later, and identify what they thought they did well and what they need to do to improve for the next lesson.

SESSIONS 12 AND 13

Introducing the handstand

(See 'Specific skills guide' – Handstand, page 222.)

Consolidation from previous session: combining movements with a change of direction and levels, and an awareness of space.

LEARNING OBJECTIVES

(The objectives of the session need to be made explicit to the children. They also need to assess the extent to which they have achieved them.)

Physical

1   To learn to perform a correct and safe handstand.

2   To use criteria to improve performance.

Well-being

3   To know some of the benefits to health and well-being of physical activity.

Broader learning

4   To remember and name particular muscle groups.

ASSESSMENT CRITERIA – QUESTIONS TO CONSIDER

1   Can the children perform a safe and correct handstand?

2   Are the children able to assess their and others' sequences against criteria, making adjustments to show improvement?

3   Can children articulate some benefits of engaging in an active lifestyle?

4   Can children name one or two muscle groups that they are developing through gymnastics activities, for example hamstring, quadriceps, calf, biceps, triceps etc.?

Warm-up

	Content	Teaching points
1	Run in and out of each other (adding changes of direction, speed, levels and pathways) and on the sound of the tambour jump once and then jump with a turn.	Highlight the use of arms in the jump to raise the centre of gravity. Keep the head upright. Verbalise responses and share ideas.

2	Run in and out of each other (adding changes of direction, speed, levels and pathways) and on the sound of the tambour roll and then change the direction of your roll. (No forward or backward rolls as there are no mats.)	Highlight good body tension to keep the body rotating – good use of core (stomach) muscles.
3	Run in and out of each other (adding changes of direction, speed, levels and pathways) and on the sound of the tambour jump once and then perform your jump at a different level.	Select one or two examples to show.
4	Run in and out of each other (adding changes of direction, speed, levels and pathways) and on the sound of the tambour jump once and then perform your jump at a different level. Then roll and change the direction of your roll.	This may need to be broken down and built back up again.
	DEVELOPING SUPPLENESS – Sit with your legs straight in front. Gently press your trunk down to your legs (hold for a count of 20 and relax) – easy pressure. **DEVELOPING STRENGTH** – Take your weight on both hands and push your bottom and tucked legs into the air (five times). **QUESTIONS** – Can the children name any muscles groups that they are developing? Can they articulate some benefits of engaging in an active lifestyle?	

Floor work

As a class activity practise the preparatory stages 1 and 2 of the handstand (see 'Specific skills guide' – Handstand, page 223).

The teacher will then demonstrate the technique of the handstand (using an able child) to the whole class. The following tasks then take the class as a whole through the next stages of the handstand.

	Content	Teaching points
1	Show the following starting position: hands flat on the floor, fingers pointing forwards, shoulder width apart, head looking just in front of the fingers. One leg is bent at the knee and the other is straight behind. Then push off the bent leg and gently swing the other leg straight up.	This is in effect the end of the lunge step in the full handstand. Select a good example to show.

2	As above, but the push-off leg swings into the air as the other leg comes to the ground.	There is a feeling of legs changing places in the air. Legs are straight. Select a good example to show and allow time to practise. Some children may need to remain at this stage, but try to develop their confidence so they move on to stages 3, 4 and 5 in the second week of the session. Others can continue to develop the lunge step as in the 'Specific skills guide' – Handstand (page 224).
3	With a partner, devise a sequence where you take the weight on your hands (this might be a handstand), jump, roll or balance. Plan, practise and refine.	You may need to break this down into stages. Have several mini-plenaries where children have the opportunity to show their developing sequences, and highlight good body tension, clear body shapes and control and coordination.
4	Change the order of your actions and consider where you have shown a change in speed, levels and direction.	Have several mini-plenaries as above.
5	In pairs, show another pair your sequence.	Pairs are to feed back against the criteria above – allow children to respond to feedback by having the opportunity to develop their sequences further.

Apparatus

	Content	Teaching points
1	Select a group at a time to give more individual support on performing the handstand.	Continue to refer to the 'Specific skills guide' – Handstand (page 222).
2	Using the apparatus, adapt your sequence on to both the floor and apparatus.	Remind children of how they can wholly use the apparatus, touch more than one piece of apparatus, or touch the floor and apparatus. Also, remind them that they can vary the ways they perform, for example mirroring, matching, or working in canon or unison. Encourage peer-assessment.

Final activity

Hold a balance on three points (three body parts), move to two, move to one and then stand tall.

Classroom

Children should make a note of their sequence with their partner to use later, and identify what they thought they did well and what they need to do to improve for the next lesson.

SESSIONS 14 AND 15
Travelling and balance

Consolidation from previous session: combining taking weight on the hands, jumps, rolls and balance in a sequence that includes changes in levels , direction and speed and may include performing a handstand.

LEARNING OBJECTIVES

(The objectives of the session need to be made explicit to the children. They also need to assess the extent to which they have achieved them.)

Physical

1   To know how to change body shape within actions to add variety to a sequence.

2   To know why it is important to warm up prior to activity and how to do so.

Well-being

3   To know some of the muscles that need to be strong in order to optimise gymnastic performance.

Broader learning

4   To use gymnastic terms to describe body shapes.

ASSESSMENT CRITERIA – QUESTIONS TO CONSIDER

1   Can the children change their body shapes within actions in their sequences?

2   Are they able to lead a partner through a short warm-up and understand why they are doing so?

3   Can they identify one or two muscle groups that need to be strong and supple to maximise gymnastic performance?

4   Can the children use gymnastic vocabulary to describe each other's body shapes, for example tucked, extended, stretched, arched or piked?

Warm-up

	Content	Teaching points
1	In pairs, one partner leads a short warm-up routine.	Make sure that the intensity starts slowly and gradually increases. Try to include some of the previous actions that you have learned.
2	Change over so that the other person leads the warm-up.	Can you think of different movements and actions?

3	Discuss as a whole class why the warm-ups were effective and share examples of good warm-up activities.	Select children to demonstrate and encourage the whole class to contribute.

DEVELOPING SUPPLENESS – Sitting with your legs in front, bend one knee so the sole of your foot lies flat against your inner thigh and slowly lean forward five times, holding for 10 seconds. Change legs and repeat.

DEVELOPING STRENGTH – With front support on your hands, walk your arms around your feet. Practise press-ups from a kneeling position.

QUESTION – Which parts of the body need to be strong and supple for improved gymnastic performance?

Floor work

	Content	Teaching points
1	Practise handstands.	See 'Specific skills guide' – Handstand (page 222). The emphasis now on the lunge step preparation. Tension is essential at this stage.
2	Repeat, and when the feet touch down move straight into a jump and landing.	Prepare mentally for the second part of the phrase. Select one or two children to demonstrate and highlight key criteria.
3	When task 2 is fluent add another action to the pattern.	Allow children to get task 2 right before moving on. The next action must flow on from the landing of the jump.
4	Now work with a partner and show each other your sequence. Select which ideas you are going to use in a combined sequence. Plan, practise and refine.	Children may need support with their negotiating skills. Select one or two good examples to show that demonstrate good body tension and controlled movements. Discuss how these are achieved.
5	Now add variety to this pattern by thinking about changing body shapes.	Try to encourage children to experiment freely before arriving at a finished pattern.
6	Practise each part in turn trying different possibilities.	This will encourage clarity.
7	In pairs, show another pair your sequence.	Identify to each other how different shapes have changed what initially were quite similar phrases.

Apparatus

	Content	Teaching points
1	Using the apparatus, adapt your sequence on to both the floor and apparatus.	Do you need to adapt your body shapes to accommodate the apparatus?
2	Select pairs of children to demonstrate to the rest of the class. Make sure everyone has the opportunity to perform.	Focus the attention of the rest of the class on particular pairs and encourage them to find interesting body shapes to describe to the rest of the class.

Final activity

Try to turn your partner over – partner should resist. Tension throughout the body is needed. All lie in a stretched position and hold the stretch.

Classroom

Children should make a note of their sequence with their partner to use later, and identify what they thought they did well and what they need to do to improve for the next lesson.

SESSIONS 16 AND 17

Springing and landing with rotation

Consolidation from previous session: to add variety to a sequence by changing body shape.

LEARNING OBJECTIVES

(The objectives of the session need to be made explicit to the children. They also need to assess the extent to which they have achieved them.)

Physical

1   To know how to rotate jumping actions.

2   To consolidate springing and jumping on to and off the apparatus.

Well-being

3   To know about activities that will develop strength and suppleness.

Broader learning

4   To know that a healthy diet, adequate sleep and other factors are important in optimising sporting achievement.

ASSESSMENT CRITERIA – QUESTIONS TO CONSIDER

1   Are the children able to perform a sequence that includes jumps with rotation?

2   Can they demonstrate springing and jumping actions on to and off the apparatus?

3   Can the children suggest and perform activities that develop strength and suppleness?

4   Are they able to name some key lifestyle considerations in achieving sporting success?

Warm-up

	Content	Teaching points
1	Run in and out of each other (adding changes of direction, speed, levels and pathways) and on the sound of the tambour jump once and then change the shape of your jump, for example tuck, star or pike.	Verbalise responses and share ideas.
2	Run in and out of each other (adding changes of direction, speed, levels and pathways) and on the sound of the tambour take the weight on your hands and then move into a different body shape while still taking the weight on your hands.	Verbalise responses and share ideas. Reinforce the need for strong body tension.

	Content	Teaching points
3	Run in and out of each other (adding changes of direction, speed, levels and pathways) and on the sound of the tambour hold a balance and change your body shape while still holding the balance.	Verbalise responses and share ideas. Reinforce the need for strong body tension.
	DEVELOPING SUPPLENESS – Support your arms on the wall and stretch your legs behind. Keep one bent and straighten the other. Hold the stretch for 15 seconds and then change legs. **DEVELOPING STRENGTH** – Take your weight on your hands, bend the knees and push back to your feet – give in the arms a little, followed by an explosive push. **QUESTION** – Other than training, what other lifestyle considerations are necessary in being a successful sportsperson, for example healthy diet, adequate sleep, no alcohol or drugs (smoking)?	

Floor work

	Content	Teaching points
1	Move over the floor travelling and turning.	Verbalise the various responses and share ideas.
2	Repeat, clearly changing your turning action as you go.	Verbal commands may help here. See task 3 below for guidance.
3	Combine a pivot turn into a jumping turn and into a rolling turn.	Repeat several times to ensure a variety of responses and accurate responses. Some may add a wheeling turn (cartwheel).
4	Now work with a partner and show each other your sequence. Select which ideas you are going to use in a combined sequence and work in unison. Plan, practise and refine.	Children may need support with their negotiating skills. Encourage children initially to count out loud to facilitate the unison work. Select one or two good examples to show that demonstrate good timing, body tension and controlled movements. Discuss how this is achieved.
5	Select pairs of children to demonstrate to the rest of the class. Make sure everyone has the opportunity to perform.	The rest of the class should describe the actions and note where the pair was able to work effectively in unison.

Apparatus

Include all the boxes, the movement table and the benches.

	Content	Teaching points
1	Find places on the apparatus where you can push off from the hands and land on the floor.	Encourage children to find different appropriate places. Legs need to thrust out as arms push. Children should start in a squat position.
2	Approach run on to part of the apparatus, jump high into the air and land in control. Can you rotate the jump in the air?	The intention is for continuous action. Landings must be clear and controlled.
3	Cross any part of the apparatus just touching with the hands trying to push, and have a moment of flight.	The arms need to 'give' prior to the final push – rest of the body similarly, a recoil and explosive thrust. Select a child who can demonstrate this well. Then all practise again.
4	In your pairs, make a sequence that includes some of your rotating actions and some springing actions you have just tried.	Allow time for children to plan, practise and refine.
5	Select pairs of children to demonstrate to the rest of the class. Make sure everyone has the opportunity to perform.	Direct the attention of the class to a particular pair and encourage them to observe 'explosive' movements that they can describe to the rest of the class.

Final activity

Put the benches down to the floor. Place your feet under the benches (knees bent – important) and bring head to knees in a slow and controlled way ten times. (This is a stomach-strengthening activity and it should never be done quickly.)

Classroom

Children should make a note of their sequence with their partner to use later, and identify what they thought they did well and what they need to do to improve for the next lesson.

Specific skills: (a) headstand, (b) lunge step into round off and (c) sideways shoulder roll.

(a)

(b)

(c)

Rotation - cartwheels and different kinds of turning actions

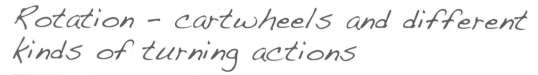

(See 'Specific skills guide' – Cartwheel, page 225.)

Consolidation from previous session: to explore rotational movements and flight (by pushing off the apparatus with the hands) and performing with a partner in unison.

LEARNING OBJECTIVES

(The objectives of the session need to be made explicit to the children. They also need to assess the extent to which they have achieved them.)

Physical

1   To learn to perform a correct and safe cartwheel.

2   To know why it is important to warm up prior to activity and how to do so.

Well-being

3   To identify which joints are affected by different stretches.

Broader learning

4   To share ideas and support one another in an encouraging, constructive way.

ASSESSMENT CRITERIA – QUESTIONS TO CONSIDER

1   Can children perform a correct and safe cartwheel?

2   Are they able to lead a partner through a short warm-up and understand why they are doing so?

3   Can the children name joints that are affected by different stretches, for example elbow, shoulder, ankle etc.?

4   Can they share ideas when planning sequences? Are they supportive when watching each other's performances, giving positive and constructive feedback?

Warm-up

	Content	Teaching points
1	In pairs, one partner leads a short warm-up routine. Include some of the turning actions learned previously, for example pivot, jumping and rolling turn.	Make sure that the intensity starts slowly and gradually increases. When jumping, use your arms to lift your centre of gravity and gain height.
2	Change over so that the other person leads the warm-up.	Can you include actions where you push off with your hands?

3	Discuss as a whole class the effectiveness of the activities, and share good examples.	Select children to demonstrate and encourage the whole class to contribute. Reiterate the importance of the warm-up.

DEVELOPING SUPPLENESS – Hold your arms above your head and slowly circle them forward ten times, and back ten times. Can you alternate with one arm moving forwards and the other one backwards? Sit down and circle your feet forward and backwards.

DEVELOPING STRENGTH – Practise handstands – children should now be confident with this activity so expect tension and stretching.

QUESTION – Which joints are affected by different stretches?

Floor work

	Content	Teaching points
1	Revise turning jumps from the last session.	Step on to the take-off leg to gain momentum. Share ideas.
2	Practise the turning jumps, taking off from one foot. Swing the free leg and arms to assist the turn. First try landing on one foot and then on two feet.	Select one or two children to show and highlight criteria.
3	Contrast this with a turning jump, taking off with two feet. First try landing on one foot and then two feet.	Initiate the turn with a strong twist in the opposite direction.
4	Combine two different turning jumps together and add a travelling action in between the two.	Emphasise the need for clear action to cross the floor into the second jump.
5	Try turning now by a wheeling action (the body looking and feeling like a wheel – arms and legs = spokes. Work with a partner and try out different ideas.	Suggest moving from feet to hands to help this feeling. Encourage children to share ideas.
6	Put together a phrase that includes a wheeling turn, a jumping turn, a pivoting turn and an action that does not turn. Plan, practise and refine.	The non-turning action need not come at the end of the phrase. Select one or two pairs to show as part of a mini-plenary and highlight criteria.
7	In pairs, show another pair your sequence.	Encourage each pair to discuss with each other what they like about the sequence and what they would like to develop further and how they might do this. Provide opportunities for this.

Apparatus

Use benches and mats – arrange for the tasks below.

The teacher will then demonstrate the technique of the cartwheel (using an able child) to the whole class. After this he/she will work with one group at a time teaching the cartwheel (see 'Specific skills guide' – Cartwheel, page 225).

The rest of the class will work as directed below, rotating as instructed by the teacher.

	Content	Teaching points
1	Group 1 – Begin to master the cartwheel.	The teacher remains at this station.
2	Group 2 – Using benches and mats, practise a wheeling turn, a jumping turn and a pivoting turn.	Encourage peer-support and -assessment.
3	Group 3 – Using mats, practise forward and backward rolls (or other rolls if unable to perform these).	Ask children while they are working what makes this kind of turn different from other turns practised.
4	Group 4 – Using benches and mats, practise run, hurdle and step jump on to the bench, immediately turning and jumping off.	Do not anticipate the turn prior to take-off (no 360° turns).
5	Group 5 – Using two mats together lengthwise, make a pattern of three turning actions that travel along the length of the mats. Try different ideas.	Remind children of the different actions already experienced.

Final activity

Hold a balance for a count of 5 and then do a turning action into another controlled balance. Sit down with good poise.

Classroom

Children should make a note of their sequence with their partner to use later, and identify what they thought they did well and what they need to do to improve for the next lesson.

SESSION 20

Assessment activity

This session will assess children's knowledge and understanding gained from the sessions throughout the year. Children should be encouraged to take responsibility for their own learning by identifying what they can achieve, what they need to do to develop and how they will do this.

LEARNING OBJECTIVES

(The objectives of the session need to be made explicit to the children. They also need to assess the extent to which they have achieved them.)

Physical

1   To perform a sequence of contrasting actions.

2   To adapt a sequence performed on the floor to include both the floor and apparatus.

3   To remember and perform the sequence with consistency, coordination and control.

Well-being

4   To know that strength and suppleness are key attributes of a gymnast.

Broader learning

5   To know how to adapt actions to accommodate individual abilities.

DISCUSSION

Discuss and share ideas of the key attributes of a gymnast and why being strong and supple is important.

Talk about what constitutes good work and how improvements can be made.

ASSESSMENT CRITERIA – QUESTIONS TO CONSIDER

1   Can the children perform contrasting actions in a sequence?

2   Can they adapt their sequence from the floor to include both the floor and apparatus?

3   Can they remember and perform the sequence with consistency, coordination and control?

4   Can the children talk about what a gymnast needs to develop physically and so improve their performance?

5   Can they adapt actions within their sequence to accommodate their individual abilities?

OUTCOME

Some children will achieve, some will excel and some will achieve less.

Warm-up

	Content	Teaching points
1	Play the Bean Game – children move around the hall according to the bean that is called out: runner bean – running; jumping bean – jumping; chilli bean – rubbing all body parts to keep warm; jelly bean – wobbling like jelly; frozen bean – being still; baked bean – lying down as if looking at the sky; butter bean – sliding on your bottom.	Verbalise the children's body actions and highlight where they are demonstrating with good control and tension.

Floor work

	Content	Teaching points
1	With a partner, plan a sequence that includes the following: a balance, jump, roll, headstand and either taking the weight on your hands and/or a handstand and/or a cartwheel.	Remind children of the diverse ways in which they can perform these actions: with varied body shapes; travelling in and out of balances; with a variety of levels, speed and direction. In the sequence consider where they will match, mirror and perform actions in canon and unison. They may need to adapt actions to accommodate each other's ability.
2	Practise and refine.	Circulate and set differentiated challenges to accommodate individual abilities. Show one or two examples and highlight the criteria above. Encourage skilful work.
3	Practise and refine, and when you can remember your sequence consider the criteria again. Do you need to make changes to develop your performance further?	Encourage children to have six different movements (although this will be dependent on ability). Ask children what they can do well and what they need to do to improve.
4	Pairs are to show (select several pairs at a time so the whole class has the opportunity to show).	Focus the children's attention on particular pairs and encourage them to identify where the criteria have been met.

Apparatus

	Content	Teaching points
1	In your pairs adapt your sequences using the floor and apparatus.	Provide opportunities for the children to show and assess these.
	ASSESSMENT – By the teacher (in conjunction with a teaching assistant where applicable), and also peer-assessment by the children. Use ICT to record as many performances as possible so the children can self-assess during the lesson and in the classroom. This can also be kept as a record of their achievement.	

Final activity

Walk around the room, stretch up high and curl up tightly. Wait to be tapped to line up (enrol some children to help).

Classroom

Children should make a note of their sequence with their partner for their records. They may use these in the next academic year.

The sessions

Year 5

SESSION 1

Assessment activity

This first session is for an initial assessment of the children's capabilities to ascertain what they know and what they can do.

This session relates to the final assessment task in Year 4.

LEARNING OBJECTIVES

(The objectives of the session need to be made explicit to the children. They also need to assess the extent to which they have achieved them.)

Physical

1   To perform a sequence of contrasting actions.

2   To adapt a sequence performed on the floor to include both the floor and apparatus.

3   To remember and perform the sequence with consistency, coordination and control.

Well-being

4   To know that strength and suppleness are key attributes of a gymnast.

Broader learning

5   To know how to adapt actions to accommodate individual abilities.

DISCUSSION

Discuss and share ideas of the key attributes of a gymnast and why being strong and supple is important.

Talk about what constitutes good work and how improvements can be made.

ASSESSMENT CRITERIA – QUESTIONS TO CONSIDER

1   Can the children perform contrasting actions in a sequence?

2   Can they adapt their sequence from the floor to include both the floor and apparatus?

3   Can they remember and perform the sequence with consistency, coordination and control?

4   Can the children talk about what a gymnast needs to develop physically and so improve their performance?

5   Can they adapt actions within their sequence to accommodate their individual abilities?

OUTCOME

Some children will achieve, some will excel and some will achieve less.

Warm-up

	Content	Teaching points
1	Play a Jump, Roll and Balance Game – the children jog around and perform the jump, roll or balance that is called out: straight jump, low level balance, log roll, star jump, scissor jump, teddy bear roll, one foot to the other etc.	Verbalise the children's body actions and highlight where they are demonstrating good control and tension.

Floor work

	Content	Teaching points
1	With a partner, plan a sequence that includes the following: a balance, jump or roll and either taking your weight on the hands and/or a handstand and/or a cartwheel.	Remind the children of the diverse ways in which they can perform these actions: with varied body shapes; travelling in and out of balances; with a variety of levels, speed and direction. In the sequence consider where they will match, mirror and perform actions in unison. They may need to adapt actions to accommodate each other's ability.
2	Practise and refine.	Circulate and set differentiated challenges to accommodate individual abilities. Show one or two examples and highlight the criteria above.
3	Practise and refine, and when you can remember your sequence, consider the criteria as in task 1 again. Do you need to make changes to develop your performance further?	Encourage children to have six different movements (although this will be dependent on ability). Ask children what they can do well and what they need to do to improve.
4	Select pairs to show (select several pairs at a time so the whole class has the opportunity to show).	Focus the children's attention on particular pairs and encourage them to identify where the criteria have been met.

Apparatus

	Content	Teaching points
1	In your pairs adapt your sequences using the floor and apparatus.	Provide opportunities for the children to show and assess these.
	ASSESSMENT – By the teacher (in conjunction with a teaching assistant where applicable), and also peer-assessment by the children. Use ICT to record as many performances as possible so the children can self-assess during the lesson and in the classroom. This can also be kept as a record of their achievement.	

Final activity

Walk around the room, stretch up high and curl up tightly. Wait to be tapped to line up (enrol some children to help).

Classroom

Children should make a note of their sequence with their partner to use later, and identify what they thought they did well and what they need to do to improve for the next lesson.

Balance - counterbalance and counter-tension

Consolidation from previous session: to perform contrasting actions in a sequence that the children can replicate on both the floor and apparatus.

LEARNING OBJECTIVES

(The objectives of the session need to be made explicit to the children. They also need to assess the extent to which they have achieved them.)

Physical

1   To learn how to perform an action with a partner involving counter-tension.

2   To continue to develop an understanding of why it is important to warm up prior to activity and how to do so.

Well-being

3   To know further activities that develop strength and suppleness.

Broader learning

4   To be able to teach an action to another person.

ASSESSMENT CRITERIA – QUESTIONS TO CONSIDER

1   Can the children perform an action with their partner using counter-tension?

2   Are the children able to lead a partner through a short warm-up and understand why they are doing so?

3   Are they able, in pairs, to share ideas of actions that develop both suppleness and strength?

4   Can they teach their action with counter-tension to another pair?

Warm-up

	Content	Teaching points
1	In pairs, one partner leads a short warm-up routine.	Make sure that the intensity starts slowly and gradually increases. Try to include some of the actions that you have learned previously.
2	Change over so that the other person leads the warm-up.	Can you think of different movements and actions? What do you need to be aware of when you are travelling around the hall?

3	Discuss as a whole class why the activities are effective and share examples.	Select children to demonstrate and encourage the whole class to contribute.
	DEVELOPING SUPPLENESS AND STRENGTH – Encourage children, in pairs, to share ideas and actions that develop both suppleness and strength. Demonstrate good examples with the whole class who then try these themselves.	

Floor work

Over the next few sessions children will be introduced to actions with counterbalance and counter-tension so that they learn a wider range of possibilities and explore more difficult and creative ways to perform when working with a partner.

It is suggested you prepare task cards (see 'Apparatus diagrams and task cards' on page 229), so that over the two-week period children can be given differentiated challenges.

	Content	Teaching points
1	With a partner, with feet together, hold each other's wrists and lean out supporting each other's weight.	Model this movement with a child or select two children to demonstrate. The children hold wrists for safety reasons. If they hold hands and one lets go, the other will fall, whereas if they hold wrists and one lets go the other will still have hold of the wrist. Explain that this is counter-tension (leaning away).
2	In this position sit down and then stand up.	Feel the need to tighten the core muscles and hold strong tension throughout the body. *There should be no need to tip backwards or forwards.* Select one or two pairs to show.
3	Stand back to back, with your feet close to your partner's. Hold hands behind and lean out.	Select one or two pairs to show. Highlight the need to plan the movement together. This is another example of counter-tension.

4	Now move your feet so that they are away from your partner's. Lean out again and try to balance on one foot.	As above.
5	Bend down and look through your legs. Hold hands and with straight legs lean out and support each other's weight.	As above.
6	Try the balance shown on your task card. When you have perfected it, teach it to another pair.	Use task cards to differentiate. Encourage children to show another pair their action and teach it to them.

Apparatus

	Content	Teaching points
1	With your partner, explore the apparatus to find where you can perform the counter-tension actions. You may need to adapt them.	In pairs, one may be on and one off the apparatus. Encourage the children to be at different levels. Select children to share ideas.

Final activity

As a class, squat jump three forward, three to the left, three to the right. Then keep in a squat position, lean forward and take the weight on your arms (shoulder width apart) and stretch one leg behind and hold for count of 10. Exchange legs and stretch.

Classroom

Children should make a note of their sequence with their partner to use later, and identify what they thought they did well and what they need to do to improve for the next lesson.

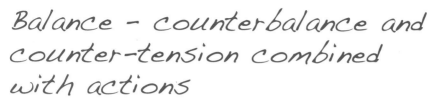

Balance – counterbalance and counter-tension combined with actions

Consolidation from previous session: to introduce performing an action with a partner involving counter-tension.

LEARNING OBJECTIVES

(The objectives of the session need to be made explicit to the children. They also need to assess the extent to which they have achieved them.)

Physical

1   To continue to learn how to perform an action involving counter-tension with a partner and learn about counterbalance.

2   To use criteria to improve their own and others' performances.

Well-being

3   To identify the changes that occur in their bodies during activity and know how this is beneficial to their health.

Broader learning

4   To be able to teach an action to another.

ASSESSMENT CRITERIA – QUESTIONS TO CONSIDER

1   Can the children perform additional actions with counter-tension with their partner, and show they understand what counterbalance is?

2   Can the children assess their own and others' performances against given criteria?

3   Are they able to identify the changes that occur to their bodies during activity and describe how this is beneficial to their health?

4   Can pairs teach their action involving counterbalance/-tension to another pair?

Warm-up

	Content	Teaching points
I	Run in and out of each other (adding changes of direction, speed, levels and pathways) and on the sound of the tambour get into pairs and, with control, show an example of counter-tension.	Verbalise responses. Select one or two pairs to show and encourage the rest of the class to try these ideas. Highlight taking the weight of their partner by leaning away from them.

2	Run in and out of each other (adding changes of direction, speed, levels and pathways) and on the sound of the tambour get into pairs and perform another example of counter-tension.	As above.
	DEVELOPING SUPPLENESS – Circle your arms slowly in front of your body (a) both in the same direction, and (b) in opposite directions – pushing not swinging. **DEVELOPING STRENGTH** – Practise taking your weight on your hands, and handstands.	

Floor work

Use task cards for task 4 below, so children can be given differentiated challenges. See 'Apparatus diagrams and task cards' (page 229) for ideas.

	Content	Teaching points
1	With a partner, feet together and holding each other's shoulders, lean out supporting each other's weight (counter-tension). In this position sit down and then stand up.	Model this movement with a child or select two children to demonstrate. If you feel yourself falling forwards, lean back. Encourage children to grip shoulders.
2	Child 1: kneel down, stretching arms out to the side. Child 2: stand behind and place straight arms on your partner's shoulders, move your legs away and lean in so that you are taking your weight on your partner (counterbalance). Make sure your legs are straight.	Select one or two pairs to show. Explain the difference between counterbalance (leaning towards) and counter-tension (leaning away).

3	Explore other ways of counterbalancing.	Verbalise responses and emphasise strong body tension.
4	Try the balance shown on your task card.	Use task cards to differentiate. Encourage children to show another pair their action and teach it to them.
5	Plan a sequence that includes two different actions that show changes in body shape and two counterbalance/-tensions	Example: start with a counterbalance (task 1 above) and move into a supported handstand with legs apart (one child performing a handstand, the other holding a foot), then both move into bunny jumps that modify into becoming a tuck and stretch roll. Verbalise responses and share ideas.
6	In pairs, show another pair your sequence. Then teach each other your sequences.	You will need to pair groups carefully and give support as required.

Apparatus

	Content	Teaching points
1	In pairs, plan, perform and adapt your sequence using both the floor and apparatus.	Select children to share ideas.
2	Pairs are to show (select several pairs at a time so the whole class has the opportunity to show).	Concentrate children on different pairs and encourage them to note changes in body shapes and where counterbalance and counter-tension occur.

Final activity
Perform slow trunk curls, tucking your feet under the apparatus (ten times) – knees bent. This is stomach-strengthening. Then stand up straight.

Classroom
Children should make a note of their sequence with their partner to use later, and identify what they thought they did well and what they need to do to improve for the next lesson.

Rotation – turning into and out of balance

Consolidation from previous session: to combine actions with counterbalance and counter-tension on both the floor and apparatus.

LEARNING OBJECTIVES

(The objectives of the session need to be made explicit to the children. They also need to assess the extent to which they have achieved them.)

Physical

1   To revise moving into and out of balance with turning (learning about axes of rotation).

2   To know that accuracy, consistency and clarity of movement are key to successful performance.

Well-being

3   To identify which joints are affected by different stretches.

Broader learning

4   To share ideas and support one another in an encouraging, constructive way.

ASSESSMENT CRITERIA – QUESTIONS TO CONSIDER

1   Can the children perform controlled balances from and into other movements using turns, and do they know which axis they are turning around?

2   Can the children work on accuracy, consistency and clarity of movement in their sequence?

3   Are they able to name joints that are affected by different stretches, for example elbow, shoulder, ankle etc.?

4   Can children share ideas when planning sequences and be supportive when watching others' performances, giving positive and constructive feedback?

Warm-up

	Content	Teaching points
1	In pairs, one partner leads a short warm-up routine.	Make sure that the intensity starts slowly and gradually increases. Include some of the previous actions that you have learned.
2	Change over so that the other person leads the warm-up.	Can you think of different movements and actions? What do you need to be aware of when you are travelling around the hall?

> **DEVELOPING SUPPLENESS** – Hold your arms above your head and slowly swing forward ten times, back ten times.
>
> **QUESTION** – Which joints are affected by stretches?

Floor work

	Content	Teaching points
1	Develop a pattern or phrase of balance – travel – balance – travel – balance.	Revise and reinforce: what balance means; kinds of balance; the moment of moving 'off' balance.
2	Practise, refine and hold balances for a count of 5, so they are really defined.	Can you change your weight so you overbalance and then make a smooth transition into the next phrase?
3	Repeat and change some of the travelling actions into *turning* actions and emphasise the movement of going 'off' balance. Show turns around the vertical (up and down) and horizontal (forward and back/side to side) axes.	Revise and reinforce the different kinds of turning action (jumping and pivoting, rolling and wheeling turns). Discuss axes with the children. (*Children can be responsible for getting out mats if performing forward and/or backward rolls.*)
4	Explore possibilities of turning jumps leading into balance.	Either the landing itself becomes the balance, or the landing is used to transfer weight into a different balance.
5	Practise a pattern where you turn and jump into a balance and move 'off' balance into a roll.	Verbalise responses. Select one or two good examples to demonstrate.
6	Having examined turning jumps into balance, try other kinds of turning actions to take you to balance, for example (a) rolling – balance, (b) pivoting – balance. Try rolls around different axes.	Roll and turn into balance (hold), pivot into balance. Turn jump into balance and cartwheel into final balance.
7	With a partner, share your sequence and from both ideas develop a paired sequence that includes moving into and out of balance, then into rolls and jumps. Make sure you explore the range of movements from previous sessions.	Inform the children that they will develop their sequences over the next three sessions and perform either their sequence in assembly, in a parallel class or to another year group. Encourage consistency, accuracy and clarity of movements in their sequences.

Apparatus

	Content	Teaching points
1	In week 2 of this session children should be given the opportunity to decide whether their performance will take place on the floor or whether to adapt it on to the apparatus. If they want to use the apparatus, they will need to be given time to practise. They should also take responsibility for arrangement of the apparatus with minimum supervision.	

Final activity

In pairs, A tries to turn B over while B resists. This is a strengthening activity.

Classroom

Children should make a note of their sequence with their partner to use later, and identify what they thought they did well and what they need to do to improve for the next lesson.

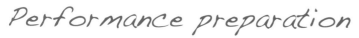

Performance preparation

Consolidation from previous session: to work on sequences that included moving into and out of balance, and into jumps and rolls.

LEARNING OBJECTIVES

(The objectives of the session need to be made explicit to the children. They also need to assess the extent to which they have achieved them.)

Physical

1   To develop a sequence against given criteria where the children choose to work on the floor or apparatus.

2   To know that accuracy, consistency and clarity of movement are key to successful performances.

Well-being

3   To identify some health and safety issues, for example the importance of wearing the correct clothing and no jewellery, of tying the hair back, of having no obstructions in the hall, and of being aware of others in the space, etc.

Broader learning

4   To evaluate each other's performances against given criteria and give feedback in a positive and constructive way.

ASSESSMENT CRITERIA – QUESTIONS TO CONSIDER

1   Can the children use criteria to develop their sequences, choosing the floor or apparatus?

2   Can they work on accuracy, consistency and clarity of movement in their sequences?

3   Are they able to verbalise some health and safety issues that they need to be aware of in gymnastics?

4   Are they able to use criteria to evaluate each other's performances and give positive and constructive feedback?

Warm-up

	Content	Teaching points
1	In groups of four, one child is to lead the others through a short warm-up routine.	Make sure that the intensity starts slowly and gradually increases. Try to include some of the actions learned previously.
2	Change over so that another child leads the warm-up. (*Over the following weeks, make sure that any child who has not led the warm-up has the opportunity to do so.*)	Can you think of different movements and actions? What do you need to be aware of when you are travelling around the hall?

3	Discuss as a whole class why the activities are effective and share examples.	Select children to demonstrate and encourage the whole class to contribute.
	DEVELOPING SUPPLENESS AND STRENGTH – Encourage children, in pairs, to share ideas and actions that develop both suppleness and strength. Demonstrate good examples with the whole class who then try these themselves.	

Floor/apparatus work

Children will continue to develop their performances from sessions 6 and 7 in preparation for performing to an audience.

	Content	Teaching points
1	With your partner, remind yourself of your sequence by practising once through. It should include moving into and out of balance, and into rolls, jumps etc. Practise and refine and hold the balances for the count of 5, so they are really defined. *Children should continue on the floor or apparatus depending on the previous decision in sessions 6 and 7.*	Children are to be responsible for getting out mats if performing forward/backward rolls, and apparatus if their performance requires this. Revise and reinforce: either the landing itself becoming the balance, or using the landing to transfer weight into different kinds of balance; the moment of moving 'off' balance.
2	Explore some other possibilities of turning jumps into balances or a pattern where you turn and jump into balance, or move off balance into a roll.	Revise and reinforce the different kinds of turning action: jumping, pivoting, wheeling (cartwheel) and rolling turns. Select one or two children to show and verbalise the criteria above.
3	Practise and refine your sequence.	Encourage children to include variety in the ways they work together: counterbalance/-tension, matching, mirroring, or working in unison and canon.
4	In pairs, show another pair your sequence.	Pairs are to feedback against criteria above – allow children opportunities to develop their sequences further based on the feedback received. Record sequences by camcorder so children can self-evaluate during the session and refine further.

Final activity

Take your weight on your hands and push to come to your feet. Repeat several times. Stand well.

Classroom

Children should make a note of their sequence with their partner to use later, and identify what they thought they did well and what they need to do to improve if the teacher decides to show these performances to others.

Springing and landing, introducing 'round-off'

(See 'Specific skills guide' – Round-off, page 226.)

Consolidation from previous session: performing a sequence as if to an audience that includes balancing into and out of jumps, rolls and actions performed with various body shapes.

LEARNING OBJECTIVES

(The objectives of the session need to be made explicit to the children. They also need to assess the extent to which they have achieved them.)

Physical

1   To learn how to 'round off' a cartwheel action.

2   To learn a range of springing actions using the apparatus, emphasising the flight phase.

Well-being

3   To gain an understanding of how muscles work.

Broader learning

4   To use given criteria to develop their work.

ASSESSMENT CRITERIA – QUESTIONS TO CONSIDER

1   Can the children 'round off' a cartwheel action?

2   Can they perform a range of actions on the apparatus that emphasise the springing and/or flight phase?

3   Are they able to describe how the muscles shorten when they are working and lengthen when relaxed?

4   Can they use given criteria to develop their work?

Warm-up

	Content	Teaching points
1	Play a Jump, Roll and Balance game – children jog around and perform the jump, roll or balance that is called out: straight jump, low-level balance, log roll, star jump, scissor jump, teddy bear roll, one foot to the other etc.	Verbalise the children's body actions and highlight where they are showing good control and tension.

	DEVELOPING SUPPLENESS – Straddle sit and press your trunk over your left leg, to the centre, over the right leg and sit straight. Repeat five times. Straighten one arm across your body and slowly pull it closer to the body – feel the stretch and hold for 10 seconds. Change arms.	
	DEVELOPING STRENGTH – Hold a front support position on hands and feet – try to clap your hands, quickly replacing your hands on the floor.	
	QUESTION – What happens to muscles when they need to 'work'?	

Floor work

	Content	Teaching points
1	Revise travelling along a straight line from feet to hands to feet.	Prepare correctly (lunge step) – work hard on the arms to hold hips high and prepare feet for landing. A twist is needed to maintain a straight line.
2	Revise the cartwheel.	See 'Specific skills guide' – Cartwheel (page 225).
3	Repeat, but at the top of the cartwheel bring your legs sharply together (stretched), then twist your hips to land facing your starting position.	This is a way to achieve a 'round-off'. Select a clear example to clarify this. The demonstrator will now be facing the direction from which he/she started. Check the new hand position (see 'Specific skills guide' – Round-off, page 227).
4	When ready, from a short approach run, skip and step into round-off.	Organise this so that those children ready for this all work towards the same direction. Those not ready continue to practise task 3.
5	Make up pattern of three springing or jumping actions to include, if possible, the round-off.	Most children will manage a form of this. Try to encourage fluency as one jump or spring leads to the next.

Apparatus

Children should be in six groups – see 'Apparatus diagrams and task cards' (page 229) for a diagram. Use task cards for this work.

	Content	Teaching points
1	Group 1 – (a) Walk along the bench, hurdle step to the springboard, and spring off to land on the mat; (b) slow run along the bench, and hurdle step to the springboard. Immediately take off and vary the shape of the jump on to the mat.	Ensure children take off from the correct part of the springboard. A chalk mark will help. Use very little knee bend to take off from the springboard (see 'Specific skills guide' – Jumping, page 217).

2	Group 2 – (a) Take two steps, and jump to swing on the rope to land on the mat; (b) take two steps, spring and grip the rope, release and land on the mat facing the place you started from.	Ensure the rope is not snaking – tension in the body. Arms should be held bent on the rope to keep the body 'alive' and not just hanging. Use a strong leg thrust and arm release for landing.
3	Group 3 – (a) Begin on the bench, take your weight on your hands and push off to the floor, rolling away from landing; (b) walk to near the top of the bench, take your weight on your hands on the stool and push off to take your feet round the stool to land on the mat.	Just as if on the floor – lunge step forward/reach forward – careful and controlled. Grip the sides of the stool with one hand at the front of the stool and one at the back (at right angles to the direction of the movement).
4	Group 4 – (a) Squat jump from the floor to the box – step and spring off on to the mat; (b) Squat jump on to the box, lie on the box, then place a hand carefully on the mat and do a forward roll.	Use hands/feet action for the squat jump. Try to get as far along the box as possible. Aim for continuity for the two actions. Strong push up into a high jump – safe and neat landing. *The teacher remains at this station until all the children have been checked for accuracy.*
5	Group 5 – (a) Practise swinging your legs from one side of the bench to the other by taking your weight on your hands, and develop by gaining flight in a second phase from the hands; (b) From the floor, squat jump on to the stool. Jump off showing a clear body shape.	Hips should be as high as possible, giving a strong thrust and swing from the initial take-off. (Revise give in the arms.) Control legs into the landing position. Give a strong push to arrive on the stool – lift the head high and hold strong tension in the jump.
6	Group 6 – Revise round-off. From a short approach run, skip and step into round-off and take into a springing action.	(See 'Specific skills guide' – Round-off, page 226.) As the body is facing the original starting place the second action needs care. A step in between the action may be needed.

Final activity

Select two children to lead the rest of the class through a range of stretching exercises. Encourage slow gradual extensions and reiterate that the best time to fully extend muscles is at the conclusion of an activity when they are really warm.

Classroom

Children should make a note of the actions and skills they still need to improve, and think how they might do this.

Travelling – with bridging

Consolidation from previous session: to learn springing and landing actions, and the 'round-off'.

LEARNING OBJECTIVES

(The objectives of the session need to be made explicit to the children. They also need to assess the extent to which they have achieved them.)

Physical

1   To learn how to make a bridged body shape on the floor and apparatus.

2   To work in a variety of ways with a partner.

Well-being

3   To use space effectively for working safely on the apparatus.

Broader learning

4   To copy another's sequence.

ASSESSMENT CRITERIA – QUESTIONS TO CONSIDER

1   Can the children make a variety of bridged body shapes and hold them with strong body tension?

2   Are they able to work in a variety of ways with their partner, including counterbalance/-tension, matching, mirroring and working in canon?

3   Can the children move between apparatus safely, avoiding others?

4   Can the children copy their partner's sequence consistently and accurately?

Warm-up

	Content	Teaching points
1	Run in and out of each other (adding changes of direction, speed, levels and pathways) and on the sound of the tambour move along an imaginary straight line from feet to hands to feet.	Prepare correctly (lunge step) – work hard on the arms to hold the hips high and prepare feet for landing. A twist is needed to maintain a straight line.
2	Run in and out of each other (adding changes of direction, speed, levels and pathways) and on the sound of the tambour perform a cartwheel.	Select one or two children to demonstrate and highlight key points (see 'Specific skills guide' – Cartwheel, page 225).

3	Run in and out of each other (adding changes of direction, speed, levels and pathways) and on the sound of the tambour repeat, but at the top of the cartwheel bring your legs sharply together (stretched), and twist your hips to land facing your starting position.	This is a way to achieve a 'round-off'. Select a clear example to clarify this. Children will now be facing the direction from which they started. Check the new hand position (see 'Specific skills guide' – Round-off, page 226).
	DEVELOPING SUPPLENESS – On your hands and knees, try to touch your knee to your forehead underneath the body and your foot to your head above the body (four times each leg). Do this slowly. **DEVELOPING STRENGTH** – Lie on your back, and raise your legs (legs bent at the knee) and chest into a 'V'-sit, then lower. Repeat six times.	

Floor work

	Content	Teaching points
1	Make a bridged shape with your body where you take your weight on your hands and feet.	Share ideas. Show how weight can be taken with the stomach facing the floor and facing the ceiling. Encourage children to try out the different versions and emphasise strong body tension.

Apparatus – climbing frame, all boxes, tables, stools and mats

Arrange apparatus as separate items. Ensure ample spacing between apparatus. Disperse children to work at a single piece of apparatus.

	Content	Teaching points
1	Use your body to bridge: floor to apparatus (or mat), across the floor from one space to another, and part of apparatus to another part.	This is an exploratory phase. Children need to have tension in order to hold bridges with control. Look for a variety of body parts in contact, a variety of body shapes created, and a variety of distances between contact points (need not be far away if height is the objective).
2	Change to a different kind of apparatus and repeat task 1 (choose a piece of apparatus close to the first piece).	Give guidance to where the children might move.
3	Now think of ways you can travel from one bridge on your first piece of apparatus to another bridge on the second piece.	Remind the children of the different kinds of actions they should be trying (rolling, springing etc.).

4	With a partner, share your movement phrase. Try each other's.	Share ideas with the class.
5	Plan a combined sequence that starts with balance – move off balance into travel into bridge.	Emphasise 'perching', then consciously going off balance. Encourage children to repeat this several times to find variety.
6	Plan a combined sequence that starts with balance – move off balance into travel into bridge, then into travel and round-off.	Encourage inclusion of variety in the way they work together in their sequence, for example counterbalance/-tension, matching, mirroring and working in canon. Select one or two pairs to show and highlight these.
7	In pairs, show another pair your sequence.	Pairs are to feed back against the criteria above – allow children further time to work on sequences so they can respond to feedback.

Final activity

Lie on your front – slowly raise your legs and head, hold for a count of 5, then lower. Repeat. This is a back strengthener. Lie on your back and stretch each part of the body fully.

Classroom

Children should make a note of their sequence with their partner to use later, and identify what they thought they did well and what they need to do to improve for the next lesson.

SESSIONS 14 AND 15

Emphasising symmetry and asymmetry

Consolidation from previous session: to make bridged body shapes and combine with actions on, across and off apparatus.

LEARNING OBJECTIVES

(The objectives of the session need to be made explicit to the children. They also need to assess the extent to which they have achieved them.)

Physical

1   To understand the difference between symmetrical and asymmetrical movements.

2   To plan and perform a sequence consistently and with control.

Well-being

3   To know some activities that stretch and strengthen muscles and joints.

Broader learning

4   To be able to teach movements and actions to others.

ASSESSMENT CRITERIA – QUESTIONS TO CONSIDER

1   Can the children perform symmetrical and asymmetrical movements when instructed?

2   Can they plan a sequence independently where actions and movements are controlled and consistent?

3   Can they share and perform exercises that strengthen and stretch muscles and joints?

4   In pairs, can the children teach their sequence to another pair?

Warm-up

	Content	Teaching points
1	Run in and out of each other (adding changes of direction, speed, levels and pathways) and on the sound of the tambour make a bridged body shape.	Verbalise responses. Select one or two children to show and encourage the rest of the class to try out the ideas. Emphasise good body extension/tension.
2	Run in and out of each other (adding changes of direction, speed, levels and pathways) and on the sound of the tambour carefully 'overbalance' into a low-level action and finish with a bridge.	Verbalise responses. Select one or two examples that show clarity of actions and good body extension/tension, and encourage the rest of the class to try the sequence.
	DEVELOPING SUPPLENESS AND STRENGTH – Encourage pairs of children to show actions that develop both suppleness and strength. Share good examples for the whole class to perform.	

Floor work

	Content	Teaching points
1	With a partner, plan a starting balance that is symmetrical and one that is asymmetrical.	Explain the terms symmetry and asymmetry. Reinforce with demonstrations. Draw attention to the difference between the two. Share ideas and encourage children to name their shape.
2	Add a jumping and springing action (for example feet to feet, or on to and from hands) where the body is symmetrical. Plan, perform and refine.	Discuss further the notion of symmetry and select one or two children to show in order to reinforce meaning.
3	Now do the same, but make your body shape asymmetrical. Plan, perform and refine.	Encourage interesting, creative body shapes and select examples to show. Encourage children to try each other's ideas.
4	Combine your symmetrical action with your asymmetrical one.	These should be two clear actions. Think about the transition from one to the other.
5	Explore starting positions where you start with your symmetrical balance, go off balance and move into an asymmetrical balance. Try several ideas and then add this to the beginning of your sequence.	Ensure that movements into and out of balance are controlled, purposeful and varied. Select one or two pairs to show.
6	In pairs, show another pair your sequence. Then teach the other pair your sequence.	You will need to pair groups carefully and give support to this as required.

Apparatus

	Content	Teaching points
1	Adapt your sequence using both the floor and apparatus. Plan, practise and refine.	Select creative, well-defined actions to show and encourage children to explore others' ideas.

Final activity

Select two children to lead the rest of the class through a range of stretching exercises. Encourage slow gradual extensions and reiterate that the best time to fully extend muscles is at the conclusion of an activity when they are really warm.

Classroom

Children should make a note of their sequence with their partner to use later, and identify what they thought they did well and what they need to do to improve for the next lesson.

Working with a partner: (a) showing symmetry and asymmetry.

Working with a partner: (b) over and under still and moving obstacles.

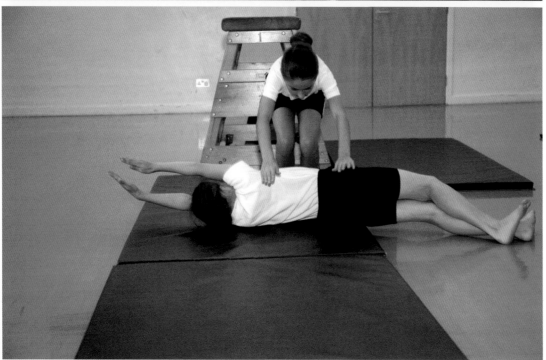

Action phrases – emphasising symmetry and asymmetry (on apparatus)

Consolidation from previous session: to explore actions with symmetry and asymmetry.

LEARNING OBJECTIVES

(The objectives of the session need to be made explicit to the children. They also need to assess the extent to which they have achieved them.)

Physical

1   To adapt actions that have symmetrical and asymmetrical shapes on to the apparatus.

2   To plan and perform a sequence consistently with control.

Well-being

3   To know some activities that stretch and strengthen muscles and joints.

Broader learning

4   To use given criteria to develop the work.

ASSESSMENT CRITERIA – QUESTIONS TO CONSIDER

1   Can the children adapt actions that have symmetrical and asymmetrical shapes on to the apparatus?

2   Can they plan a sequence independently where actions are controlled and performed with clarity?

3   Can they identify activities that stretch and strengthen muscles and joints?

4   Are they able to use given criteria to develop their work?

Warm-up

	Content	Teaching points
1	In groups of four, one child is to lead the others through a short warm-up routine.	Make sure that the intensity starts slowly and gradually increases. Try to include some of the previous actions that you have learned.
2	Change over so that another child leads the warm-up.	Include those who have not yet led on this activity. Can you think of different movements and actions? What do you need to be aware of when you are travelling around the hall?

	DEVELOPING SUPPLENESS AND STRENGTH – Encourage pairs of children to show actions that develop both suppleness and strength. Share good examples for the whole class to perform.	

Floor work

	Content	Teaching points
1	Make sure you are with the partner you were working with last week and practise your previous lesson's sequence that included symmetrical and asymmetrical movements.	Verbalise responses and support diligent practice.
2	Can you add a further action to your sequence? Practise and refine.	Select pairs of children to show, and encourage children to explore actions seen in their sequence. Explain that this can be called an action phrase as well as a sequence.
3	Check if your phrase includes counterbalance/-tension, places where you match, mirror and/or work in canon.	Select pairs of children to show, and encourage the class to try some of these ideas.
4	Select pairs of children to demonstrate to the rest of the class. Make sure everyone has the opportunity to perform.	Focus the children's attention on one particular pair and encourage them to look at whether the sequence shows actions performed symmetrically and asymmetrically, and whether these are clearly defined and extended.

Apparatus

Use all benches, box tops, low nestling tables etc., with mats spaced evenly around the hall.

	Content	Teaching points
1	Find ways of bridging from floor to bench (or mat to bench, or mat to floor) with (a) a symmetrical body line, and (b) an asymmetrical body line.	Check that children fully understand the differences.
2	Pick out several ideas shown and all practise.	The teacher selects ideas to show and identifies why this was done (for example, hands and head on mat – one foot on bench – is it symmetrical or asymmetrical?).

3	Experiment with crossing the bench or apparatus with (a) a symmetrical body shape, and (b) an asymmetrical body shape.	Expect skilful interpretations and good quality.
4	Some try moving along the bench as above. Others use a mat to practise moving where the actions are symmetrical, then where they are asymmetrical, leading into an asymmetrical balance (and vice versa).	If necessary children can touch the floor as they move along. Encourage children to explore bridges, rotation and cartwheels and to be quite free in second part of task. Select children to share ideas with the class.
5	Develop an action phrase based on bridging, balancing and travel – showing symmetry and asymmetry.	Children are to select ideas already practised.
6	Select children to demonstrate (several at a time).	Encourage children to feed back on whether others have included some of the above criteria.

Final activity
Select two children to lead the rest of the class through a range of stretching exercises. Encourage slow gradual extensions and reiterate that the best time to fully extend muscles is at the conclusion of an activity when they are really warm.

Classroom
Children should make a note of their final action phrase, and identify what they thought they did well and what they need to do to improve for the next lesson.

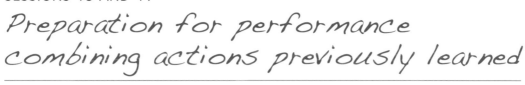

SESSIONS 18 AND 19

Preparation for performance combining actions previously learned

Consolidation from previous session: to adapt actions that are symmetrical and asymmetrical from the floor on to the apparatus.

LEARNING OBJECTIVES

(The objectives of the session need to be made explicit to the children. They also need to assess the extent to which they have achieved them.)

Physical

1   To revise previously learned actions – bridge, counterbalance/-tension, cartwheels, round-off etc. – and include them in a sequence.

2   To know that accuracy, consistency and clarity of movement are key to successful performances.

Well-being

3   To identify which joints are affected by different stretches.

Broader learning

4   To share ideas and support one another in an encouraging, constructive way.

ASSESSMENT CRITERIA – QUESTIONS TO CONSIDER

1   Do the children use previously learned actions in their sequences?

2   Do they know that accuracy, consistency and clarity of movement are key to successful performances?

3   Are they able to name joints that are affected by different stretches, for example elbow, shoulder, ankle etc.?

4   Can children share ideas when planning sequences, and be supportive when watching other performances, giving positive and constructive feedback?

Warm-up

	Content	Teaching points
1	Get into the same groups of four as in the previous warm-up session. One of the two who didn't lead the warm-up in the previous week are to lead the others through a short routine.	Make sure that the intensity starts slowly and gradually increases. Try to include some of the previous actions that you have learned.

2	Change over so that the final child leads the warm-up.	Can you think of different movements and actions? What do you need to be aware of when you are travelling around the hall?
	DEVELOPING SUPPLENESS AND STRENGTH – Encourage pairs of children to show actions that develop both suppleness and strength. Share good examples for the whole class to perform. **QUESTION** – Which joints are affected by stretches?	

Floor work

	Content	Teaching points
1	In pairs, experiment with starting positions to a sequence that shows either counterbalance or counter-tension, and that then moves off balance into a jump.	Verbalise responses and select one or two children to show.
2	Add a roll that goes into a bridge or vice versa. Perform and refine.	Verbalise responses and select one or two children to show.
3	Add an action where you spring up, and then add a cartwheel/handstand or an action where you 'round off'. Perform and refine.	Make sure you have symmetrical and asymmetrical actions in your sequence.
4	Explore changing the order of your actions and make sure they include times where you work in some of these ways with your partner: mirroring, matching and working in canon and unison. Plan, practise and refine.	Select one or two to show, and highlight clarity of actions, smooth transitions and strong body tension and extension.
5	Children will spend these two sessions refining their sequences in preparation for performing to an audience. They should use: self-, peer- and teacher assessment to evaluate and develop their sequences. ICT should support this.	

Final activity

Select two children to lead the rest of the class through a range of stretching exercises. Encourage slow gradual extensions and reiterate that the best time to fully extend muscles is at the conclusion of an activity when they are really warm.

Classroom

Children should make a note of their sequence with their partner to use later, and identify what they thought they did well and what they need to do to improve for the performance in the next session.

SESSION 20
Assessment activity

This session will assess children's knowledge and understanding gained from the sessions throughout the year. Children should be encouraged to take responsibility for their own learning by identifying what they can achieve, what they need to do to develop and how they will do this.

LEARNING OBJECTIVES

(The objectives of the session need to be made explicit to the children. They also need to assess the extent to which they have achieved them.)

Physical

1   To perform a sequence of contrasting actions.

2   To adapt a sequence performed on the floor to include both the floor and apparatus.

3   To remember and perform the sequence with consistency, coordination and control.

Well-being

4   To know that strength and suppleness are key attributes of a gymnast.

Broader learning

5   To know how to adapt actions to accommodate individual abilities.

DISCUSSION

Discuss and share ideas of the key attributes of a gymnast and why being strong and supple is important.

Talk about what constitutes good work and how improvements can be made.

ASSESSMENT CRITERIA – QUESTIONS TO CONSIDER

1   Can the children perform contrasting actions in a sequence?

2   Can they adapt their sequence from the floor to include both the floor and apparatus?

3   Can they remember and perform the sequence with consistency, coordination and control?

4   Can the children talk about what a gymnast needs to develop physically and so improve their performance?

5   Can they adapt actions within their sequence to accommodate their individual abilities?

OUTCOME

Some children will achieve, some will excel and some will achieve less.

Warm-up

	Content	Teaching points
1	Play a gymnastic action game – children jog around and perform the jump, roll or balance, handstand, cartwheel etc. that is called out, for example: straight jump, low-level balance, log roll, star jump, scissor jump, teddy bear roll, one foot to the other etc.	Verbalise the children's body actions and highlight where they are demonstrating with good control and tension. Encourage children to have a turn at being the 'caller'.

Floor work

	Content	Teaching points
1	With your partner, rehearse your performance sequence (from the previous sessions). Identify one part where you could develop it further, and practise and refine.	For example: varied body shapes; smoother transition in and out of balances; increased variety of levels, speed and direction; greater range in the way they perform; matching, mirroring, in unison and in canon. They may need to adapt actions to accommodate each other's ability.
2	Practise and refine.	Circulate and set differentiated challenges to accommodate individual abilities. Show one or two examples and highlight the criteria above.

Apparatus

	Content	Teaching points
1	In your pairs adapt your sequences using the floor and apparatus.	Provide opportunities for the children to show and assess them.
2	Select pairs to demonstrate (several at a time).	Encourage children to feed back on whether children have included some of the above criteria. Children are to record responses when they return to the classroom.
	ASSESSMENT– By the teacher (in conjunction with a teaching assistant where applicable), and also peer-assessment by the children. Use ICT to record as many performances as possible, so the children can self-assess during the lesson and in the classroom. This can also be kept as a record of their achievement.	

Final activity

Select two children to lead the rest of the class through a range of stretching exercises. Encourage slow gradual extensions and reiterate that the best time to extend muscles fully is at the conclusion of an activity when they are really warm.

Performance

Consider how the children's work might be shown to a wider audience.

The sessions

Year 6

Assessment activity

This first session is for an initial assessment of the children's capabilities to ascertain what they know and what they can do.

This session relates to the final assessment task in Year 5.

LEARNING OBJECTIVES

(The objectives of the session need to be made explicit to the children. They also need to assess the extent to which they have achieved them.)

Physical

1   To perform a sequence of contrasting actions.

2   To adapt a sequence performed on the floor to include both the floor and apparatus.

3   To remember and perform the sequence with consistency, coordination and control.

Well-being

4   To know that strength and suppleness are key attributes of a gymnast.

Broader learning

5   To know how to adapt actions to accommodate individual abilities.

DISCUSSION

Discuss and share ideas of the key attributes of a gymnast and why being strong and supple is important.

Talk about what constitutes good work and how improvements can be made.

ASSESSMENT CRITERIA – QUESTIONS TO CONSIDER

1   Can the children perform contrasting actions in a sequence?

2   Can they adapt their sequence from the floor to include both the floor and apparatus?

3   Can they remember and perform the sequence with consistency, coordination and control?

4   Can the children talk about what a gymnast needs to develop physically and so improve their performance?

5   Can they adapt actions within their sequence to accommodate their individual abilities?

OUTCOME

Some children will achieve, some will excel and some will achieve less.

Warm-up

	Content	Teaching points
1	Play a gymnastic action game – children jog around and perform the jump, roll or balance, handstand, cartwheel etc. that is called out, for example: straight jump, low-level balance, log roll, star jump, scissor jump, teddy bear roll, one foot to the other etc.	Verbalise the children's body actions and highlight where they are demonstrating with good control and tension. Encourage children to have a turn at being the 'caller'.

Floor work

	Content	Teaching points
1	Work with a partner to find a starting position to a sequence that shows either counterbalance or counter-tension, and that then moves off balance into a jump.	Counterbalance – lean towards. Counter-tension – lean away. Verbalise responses and select one or two children to show.
2	Add a roll that goes into a bridge or vice versa. Perform and refine.	Circulate and set differentiated challenges to accommodate individual abilities. Show one or two examples and highlight strong body tension and clarity of movement.
3	Add an action where you spring up, and then add a cartwheel or handstand or an action where you 'round off'. Perform and refine.	Is it possible to have actions that have symmetrical and asymmetrical shapes in your sequence? Model or select a child to demonstrate actions.
4	Explore changing the order of your actions and make sure they include times where you work in some of these ways: mirroring, matching and in unison and canon. Plan, practise and refine.	Provide opportunities for the children to show and assess them.
5	Select pairs to demonstrate (several at a time).	Encourage children to feed back on whether children have included some of the above criteria. Children are to record their responses when they return to the classroom.
	ASSESSMENT – By the teacher (in conjunction with a teaching assistant where applicable), and also peer-assessment by the children. Use ICT to record as many performances as possible so the children can self-assess during the lesson and in the classroom. This can also be kept as a record of their achievement.	

Final activity

Select two children to lead the rest of the class through a range of stretching exercises. Encourage slow gradual extensions and reiterate that the best time to extend muscles fully is at the conclusion of an activity when they are really warm.

Classroom

Children should make a note of their sequence with their partner to use later, and identify what they thought they did well and what they need to do to improve for the next lesson.

Rotation – twisting and turning

Consolidation from previous session: to perform a sequence with a partner that includes the following actions: counterbalance, counter-tension, bridge and cartwheel with round-off landing.

LEARNING OBJECTIVES

(The objectives of the session need to be made explicit to the children. They also need to assess the extent to which they have achieved them.)

Physical

1   To perform twisting and rotating actions that lead into another action.
2   To know a variety of body parts that can be used as a base for a rotating and/or twisting action.

Well-being

3   To know why it is important to warm up prior to activity and how to do so.

Broader learning

4   To work safely in a space.

ASSESSMENT CRITERIA – QUESTIONS TO CONSIDER

1   Can children perform a twisting and rotating action that leads into jump, roll etc.?
2   Can they use a variety of body parts to support rotating and twisting actions?
3   Can the children lead a warm-up with a small group of their peers, showing that they understand the importance of being prepared for activity?
4   Are the children aware of others and equipment when they travel around the hall?

Warm-up

	Content	Teaching points
1	In pairs, one partner leads a short warm-up routine.	Make sure that the intensity starts slowly and gradually increases. Include some of the previous actions that you have learned. Ask the children why it is important to warm up.
2	Change over so that the other person leads the warm-up.	Can you think of different movements and actions? What do you need to be aware of when you are travelling around the hall?
	DEVELOPING SUPPLENESS AND STRENGTH – Encourage children in their groups to plan and perform actions that develop both suppleness and strength and then share with the rest of the class for the whole class to perform.	

Floor work

	Content	Teaching points
1	With a partner, work at a low level and find different ways of travelling, with a twist beginning each new action.	Reiterate, for example twist – roll, twist – hands and feet action. Select one or two children to show.
2	Begin on your knees – fix them firmly as the base – twist your arms and shoulders round as far as they will go, then continue moving in that direction. Explore how you can perform this with your partner.	It is important to hold the base fixed as long as possible (not swivelling) and then follow in the direction of the twist. It is likely to be a rolling action following the twist. Encourage children to work in a variety of ways, for example in unison and canon, mirroring or matching.
3	Explore this action with your partner using a variety of bases.	Verbalise responses. Select one or two children to show, and highlight different ways of working.
4	Repeat (using different bases), but this time ensure that the resultant action is a turning action.	That is, use a twist to initiate a turn. Reiterate different kinds of turn (see Year 4, sessions 16 and 17 and sessions 18 and 19).
5	Go up into a handstand – twist your hips and bring your feet down in a new direction – let this lead into a turning action. Perform this with your partner in unison and canon.	A demonstration will help here – legs together to finish will also help. Encourage children who are unable to perform a handstand to take their weight on their hands – twist the hips and bring the feet down in a new direction.
6	From feet fixed as a base, twist to take your weight on your hands (the body changes direction as it twists and turns). Explore each other's ideas.	Begin in squat and gradually increase the size of the action. Discuss how the twist takes the body into a turning action in the direction of the original twist.
7	Begin on your feet, twist the top half of the body, bend the knees slightly, let the twist uncoil and use the recoil to take you into a turning jump. Explore each other's ideas.	This is an example of how the recoil effect of a twist takes the body away from the direction of the twist.
8	With your partner, use ideas 1–7 and now make an sequence of twists into turns, including jumping, rolling, balancing and a handstand (taking weight on hands).	Select one or two pairs to show. You may need to break this down for some children.
9	In pairs, show another pair your sequence. Then teach each other parts of your sequence.	You will need to organise the two pairs carefully and give support as required.

| 10 | Work together as a four on a group sequence that includes some of the actions from both of the sequences. | Encourage children to work in a variety of ways, for example mirroring, matching and working in canon or unison. Start at different times, together and apart. |

Apparatus

	Content	Teaching points
1	In your groups adapt your movement on to the apparatus. Perform, practise and refine.	Encourage the children to choose their own apparatus and design the layout. *Make sure it is safe before they use it.*
2	Each group is to show the rest of the class.	Focus groups watch each other and feed back on the different body parts used as bases.

Final activity

Each week, select two children to lead the final warm-down. This may include some strengthening activities, followed by stretching, which they will have learned in Year 5. See also the previous session.

Classroom

Children should make a note of their group sequence to use later, and identify what they thought they did well and what they need to do to improve for the next session.

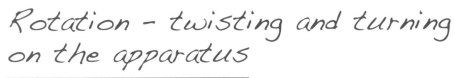

Rotation – twisting and turning on the apparatus

(A CD player, iPod station or similar will be needed for this session.)

Consolidation from previous session: to perform twisting and turning actions using a variety of body parts as a base, in pairs and small groups.

LEARNING OBJECTIVES

(The objectives of the session need to be made explicit to the children. They also need to assess the extent to which they have achieved them.)

Physical

1   To perform twisting and rotating actions that lead into another action, on both the floor and apparatus, and to begin to work with music.

2   To perform actions in a sequence with varied speeds.

Well-being

3   To know why it is important to warm up prior to activity and how to do so.

Broader learning

4   To use given criteria to develop movements and improve performance.

ASSESSMENT CRITERIA – QUESTIONS TO CONSIDER

1   Can children perform a twisting and rotating action that leads into jump, roll etc., on both the floor and apparatus, and begin to work with music?

2   Can children perform actions in a sequence with contrasting speed?

3   Can the children lead a warm-up with a small group of their peers, showing they understand the importance of being prepared for activity?

4   Can the children use given criteria to develop movements and improve performance?

Warm-up

	Content	Teaching points
I	In groups of four, one is to lead the others through a short warm-up.	Include some of the previous actions that you have learned: twisting, turning, from a variety of bases into jumps, rolls etc. Verbalise responses. How should we warm the body up?

2	Change over so that another person leads the warm-up.	Can you think of different movements and actions? What do you need to be aware of when you are travelling around the hall?
	DEVELOPING SUPPLENESS AND STRENGTH – Encourage children in their groups to plan and perform actions that develop both suppleness and strength and then share some of the ideas with the rest of the class for the whole class to perform. **QUESTION** – Why do we need to warm up before activity?	

Floor work

	Content	Teaching points
1	Get into the same groups of four from the previous session and go through the sequence that you developed in the last session. Practise and refine.	Encourage children to use their notes from the previous session. Select one or two groups to show, and highlight strong body tension and controlled actions.

Apparatus

	Content	Teaching points
1	Break back into pairs and find places on the apparatus where you can begin together (gripping apparatus), twist to leave the apparatus and roll away.	Encourage different starting positions. Verbalise responses.
2	Start together, twist and turn to arrive *against* the apparatus and synchronise your movements.	Begin far enough away for this to be possible. Which direction do you need to face to begin?
3	One begins on the apparatus one on the floor in matching balances. Twist and turn from the balance to exchange places. Find other ways of doing this same task. Vary the speed in which you perform your twist, turns and rotating movements.	The action in between the balances need not necessarily match. Start at different places – use different balances and different travelling actions.
4	Somewhere in the phase, include a handstand with a twist to land.	Select one or two children to demonstrate.
5	Back into fours, one pair shows the other pair their sequence. Then teach each other parts of your sequence.	Can you now see if your sequence can display contrast of speed?

6	Work together on a group sequence that includes some of the actions from both of the sequences.	Encourage children to work in a variety of ways, for example mirroring, matching and working in canon or unison. Start at different times, together or apart.
7	Listen to the music, then see if you can synchronise some of your actions to the different beats and show contrast in the speed that you perform your work.	Select one or two examples to show effective use of the music. (See 'The place of music', page 14.)
8	Each group is to show the rest of the class.	Focus attention on contrasting speeds in the work.

Final activity

As previous session.

Classroom

Children should make a note of their group sequence to use later, and identify what they thought they did well and what they need to do to improve for the next lesson.

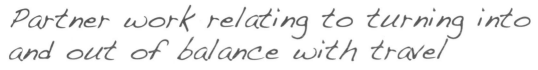

Partner work relating to turning into and out of balance with travel

Consolidation from previous session: to perform twisting and turning actions using a variety of body parts as a base on the apparatus, in pairs and small groups.

LEARNING OBJECTIVES

(The objectives of the session need to be made explicit to the children. They also need to assess the extent to which they have achieved them.)

Physical

1   To negotiate obstacles when performing actions.

2   To know how to time actions to work successfully with a partner.

Well-being

3   To identify which joints are affected by different stretches.

Broader learning

4   To assess each other's skills and plan a sequence accordingly.

ASSESSMENT CRITERIA – QUESTIONS TO CONSIDER

1   Are the children able to plan and perform actions where they use each other as an obstacle and perform actions either over, under or through etc.?

2   Can they time their actions to move safely and fluently with their partner in a sequence?

3   Are they able to name joints that are affected by different stretches, for example elbow, shoulder, ankle etc.?

4   Are they able to adapt their actions to cater for each other's ability?

Warm-up

	Content	Teaching points
1	In groups of four, one child (who didn't lead on the previous session) is to lead the others through a short warm-up.	Include some of the previous actions that you have learned: twisting, turning, from a variety of bases into jumps, rolls etc. Verbalise responses. How should we warm the body up?
2	Change over so that another person (who didn't lead on the previous session) leads the warm-up.	Can you think of different movements and actions? Remind them of the handstand action performed with a twist to land.

> **DEVELOPING SUPPLENESS AND STRENGTH** – Encourage children in their groups to plan and perform actions that develop both suppleness and strength and then share some of the ideas with the rest of the class for the whole class to perform. Can they name the muscle groups and joints they are stretching?

Floor work

Obstacles can be still or moving. Partners can negotiate with and without contact.

	Content	Teaching points
1	With a partner, A holds a balance and B finds turning actions to go over, under, round, through etc. Then reverse roles.	Encourage children to explore a range of ideas. Verbalise creative responses. Select pairs to show. No contact at this stage.
2	A holds a tucked balance. B practises turning jumps to negotiate (i.e. to move over the partner who is still). Then reverse roles.	Ensure children prepare for the jump carefully and know where they will land.
3	As in task 2, but now use a *feet – hands – feet* turning action to negotiate or get over the partner. Then reverse roles.	A long stretch will be needed to get over the obstacle as in preparation for a cartwheel – the lunge position is essential. Control and care are important.
4	Taking turns, find a balance with a space between body and floor for the partner to do rolling turns under or through.	They need to stretch high and away from the floor. Care is needed with legs as the obstacle is negotiated – they may need to be tucked into the body.
5	Develop a sequence of two actions where A is the obstacle and B turns to negotiate. Then B is the obstacle and A turns to negotiate.	As B finishes the first action he/she becomes the obstacle. A tries to make the movement from the first balance part of the preparation for the turning action over B. Again, children must explore a range of possibilities first before moulding them into sequence. Continuity is difficult to achieve – it merits some time being given to it.
6	Now try out some activities where the obstacle *slowly* moves in a clear action across the floor and the other goes over or under the obstacle.	Verbalise the responses. Select some pairs to show and encourage all the children to try out the ideas.
7	One partner tries a slow stretched rolling obstacle – in what different ways can this be negotiated by the other partner? Try it moving from and towards the partner.	Select one or two pairs to show, and highlight stretched, strong body tension. Emphasise the importance of timing.

8	Repeat with a tucked rolling obstacle.	Select one or two pairs to show, and highlight strong body tension and the importance of timing.
9	Develop a sequence of four actions: A obstacle, B negotiates; B obstacle, A negotiates (repeated). In the sequence have the obstacle moving twice, and in balance (still) twice.	This will need time – especially if fluency is to be developed. Encourage simplicity, clarity and quality. Consider introducing music for this. If you do, it will need more time.
10	In pairs show another pair your sequence.	Children are to watch each other's sequences and feed back on whether children have held clear body shapes, and have demonstrated good timing.

Apparatus

	Content	Teaching points
1	Encourage pairs to explore where they can adapt their actions on to the apparatus.	Select good examples and encourage all children to try out ideas.

Final activity
As sessions 2 and 3.

Classroom
Children should make a note of their sequence with their partner to use later, and identify what they thought they did well and what they need to do to improve for the next lesson.

Partner work – contact with obstacles related to balance, and performance preparation

Consolidation from previous session: to work in pairs to perform actions using each other as obstacles (still and moving).

LEARNING OBJECTIVES

(The objectives of the session need to be made explicit to the children. They also need to assess the extent to which they have achieved them.)

Physical

1   To use an obstacle to balance against.

2   To be able to combine a range of actions in a sequence with control and consistency.

Well-being

3   To gain further understanding of how muscles work.

Broader learning

4   To assess each other's skills and plan a sequence accordingly.

ASSESSMENT CRITERIA – QUESTIONS TO CONSIDER

1   Can children use their partner to support their balance?

2   Can they replicate a sequence of actions that they have planned that demonstrates strong body control?

3   Can children describe how muscles shorten when they are working together and lengthen when they relax?

4   Are they able to adapt their actions to cater for each other's ability?

Warm-up

	Content	Teaching points
I	Run in and out of each other (adding changes of direction, speed, levels and pathways) and on the sound of the tambour hold a balance on a large part of your body and move the balance on to a small body part.	Verbalise responses. Expect control into the balance.

2	Run in and out of each other (adding changes of direction, speed, levels and pathways) and on the sound of the tambour hold a balance on a small body part and move the balance on to a large body part.	Select one or two children to show, and highlight strong body tension.
3	With your previous week's partner, go through some of the actions where you use each other as still and moving obstacles. Try out some new ideas.	Select children to show, and encourage children to try out each other's ideas.
	DEVELOPING SUPPLENESS AND STRENGTH – Encourage children in their groups to plan and perform actions that develop both suppleness and strength and then share some of the ideas with the rest of the class for the whole class to perform. Can they name the muscle groups and joints they are stretching? How do muscles work? Do they shorten when they are working or when relaxed? Discuss.	

Floor work

	Content	Teaching points
1	In twos, explore how you can use each other as a support for the other to balance against (remember some of the counterbalance ideas previously used).	(See Year 5, sessions 2 and 3 and sessions 4 and 5.) Verbalise responses and select one or two to demonstrate. Emphasise the importance of the obstacle acting as a strong, firm base. Can one part of the body be on the partner instead of the floor?
2	With care, find an action that will take you towards your partner (the obstacle) and into the balance (as in task 1). Change roles.	For example, rolling into the balance, jumping into the balance, or wheeling into the balance. Allow time for the children to explore.
3	Put together the following: A holds a strong obstacle position/B moves into balance against A; B holds the balance then moves away and becomes a strong obstacle; A then moves towards B and holds a balance against B. Plan, practise and refine.	The movement into and out of the balances must be as important as the balance. Select examples that highlight this.
	Year 6 children should be working on longer sequences. The remainder of this session and sessions 10 and 11 are designed to enable the children to work on a performance that they can show to an audience (in assembly, to a parallel class, or to another year group).	

4	Continue to work on the above and explore how A can turn out of balance. Remind them of previous sessions where they used twists to come out of balance. Practise and refine.	An example could be the handstand, where they twist the hips and bring the feet down in new direction, or from a foot balance twist to take their weight on to the hands (the body changes direction as it twists and turns). Share ideas.
5	Add a travelling action and a roll. Practise and refine.	Verbalise responses and share ideas. Consider how you are working together with your partner and make sure you have variety in this, for example mirroring, matching and working in canon or unison. Start at different times, together and apart.
6	In pairs, show another pair your sequence. Then teach each other parts of your sequence.	You will need to organise the two pairs carefully and give support as required. You may wish again to include music at this stage or in the next task.
7	Work together on a group sequence that includes some of the actions from each of the sequences.	Encourage children to work in a variety of ways, for example mirroring, matching, working in canon or unison. Start at different times, together and apart.

Apparatus

1	In week 2 of this session, children should be given the opportunity to decide whether their performance will take place on the floor or whether to adapt it on to the apparatus. If they want to use the apparatus they will need to be given time to practise. They should also take responsibility for arrangement of the apparatus with minimum supervision.

Final activity
As sessions 2 and 3.

Classroom
Children should make a note of their group sequence to use later, and identify what they thought they did well and what they need to do to improve for the next lesson.

Performance preparation

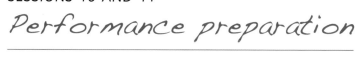

Consolidation from previous session: to use obstacles for balancing, and to plan a sequence that includes previous Year 6 content.

LEARNING OBJECTIVES

(The objectives of the session need to be made explicit to the children. They also need to assess the extent to which they have achieved them.)

Physical

1   To develop a sequence against criteria to perform to an audience.

2   To know that accuracy, consistency and clarity of movement are key to successful performances.

Well-being

3   To know why warming up and cooling down are important.

Broader learning

4   To be able to negotiate, share ideas and work with others to devise a sequence of actions.

ASSESSMENT CRITERIA – QUESTIONS TO CONSIDER

1   Can the children use criteria to develop their sequence in preparation for performance?

2   Can they work on accuracy, consistency and clarity of movement in their sequences?

3   Are children aware of the benefits of warming up and cooling down before and after activity?

4   Can children negotiate, share ideas and work with others to plan a final performance?

Warm-up

	Content	Teaching points
1	In groups of four, one is to lead the others through a short warm-up routine.	Make sure that the intensity starts slowly and gradually increases. Try to include some of the actions learned previously.
2	Change over so that another child leads the warm-up. (*Make sure any child who has not led the warm-up has the opportunity to do so.*)	Can you think of different movements and actions? Why do we warm up? Rehearse knowledge already gained.
3	Discuss as a whole class why the activities are effective and share examples.	Select children to demonstrate and encourage the whole class to contribute.

| | **DEVELOPING SUPPLENESS AND STRENGTH** – Encourage children, in pairs, to share ideas and actions that develop both suppleness and strength. Demonstrate good examples with the whole class who then try these themselves. |

Floor/apparatus work

Children will continue to develop their performances from sessions 8 and 9 in preparation for performing to an audience.

	Content	Teaching points
1	In your fours discuss and remind yourselves of your sequence by practising one or two times through. It should include use of static, moving obstacles and obstacles as support, twists and turns, a travel and a roll. Practise and refine and hold the balances for the count of 5, so they are really defined. Children should continue on the floor or apparatus depending on their previous decision in sessions 8 and 9.	*Children should be responsible for getting out mats if performing forward/backward rolls and apparatus if their performance requires this.* Revise and reinforce: solid bases to support each others' balances; stretched, strong bodies where appropriate; the importance of timing; and variety in *how* you work in your group – for example in pairs, individually, three matching and one contrasting etc. Allow plenty of time to practise and include mini-plenaries, where one group shows and highlights aspects described above.
2	Show your sequence to another group.	Groups are to feed back against the criteria listed above.
3	Use the feedback you have been given to develop your sequence further. This may include changing levels and speed in your sequence. Practise and refine.	Move around and support groups, giving formative feedback and differentiating requirements. Any children not participating and/or a teaching assistant can record sequences, and groups can self-assess.
4	Groups are to show each other in preparation for their performance to others.	Children should make brief notes of their sequences to complete when they return to classroom.

Final activity

As sessions 2 and 3.

Check: why is it important to warm down?

Classroom

Children continue to make a note of their group sequence to use later, and identify what they thought they did well and what they may need to do to improve for a performance to others.

SESSIONS 12 AND 13

Further development of basic skills

Consolidation from previous session: to perform a group sequence consisting of using obstacles as support, to go over, under etc., twisting and turning actions, travel and roll.

LEARNING OBJECTIVES

(The objectives of the session need to be made explicit to the children. They also need to assess the extent to which they have achieved them.)

Physical

1   To be able to develop actions against given criteria.

2   To know that accuracy, consistency and clarity of movement are key to successful performances.

Well-being

3   To understand about how activity contributes to a healthy lifestyle.

Broader learning

4   To know how to give feedback in a positive and constructive manner.

ASSESSMENT CRITERIA – QUESTIONS TO CONSIDER

1   Can the children use criteria to develop their actions?

2   Can they work on accuracy, consistency and clarity of movement in their sequences?

3   Can children describe some ways in which activity will support their lifestyle?

4   Do children provide feedback in a positive and constructive manner to one another?

Warm-up

	Content	Teaching points
1	In groups of four, one child leads the others through a short warm-up routine.	Make sure that the intensity starts slowly and gradually increases. Try to include some of the previous actions learned.
2	Change over so that another child leads the warm-up. (*Make sure any child who has not led the warm-up has the opportunity to do so.*)	Can you think of different movements and actions? Why do we warm up?

3	Discuss as a whole class how being active contributes to a healthy lifestyle.	Expect responses relating to (a) physical development, including that of the muscles and heart, mobility of joints, strength, suppleness, speed, stamina etc.; (b) motor skill development: stability, locomotion etc.; (c) social development: negotiating, sharing ideas, working together etc.; and (d) cognitive development: planning ideas etc.
	DEVELOPING SUPPLENESS AND STRENGTH – Encourage children, in pairs, to share ideas and actions that develop both suppleness and strength. Demonstrate good examples with the whole class who then try these themselves.	

Floor work

	Content	Teaching points
1	With a partner, revise an action where you take your weight on your hands.	Perform it in unison or canon, matching or mirroring. Verbalise responses and select one or two to demonstrate.
2	Find a travelling action that leads into your action.	Start together or at different times. Verbalise responses and select one or two to demonstrate.
3	Travel into and out of your action.	Finish together. Verbalise responses and select one or two to demonstrate.

Apparatus

Children should be in eight groups (select five or six apparatus arrangements to suit your situation and arrange accordingly). See 'Apparatus diagrams and task cards' (page 229) for guidance. Use task cards for this session.

Children should be encouraged to peer-assess against given criteria in a supportive manner and be given sufficient time to master these tasks and achieve quality.

	Content	Teaching points
1	Group 1 – Perform a backward roll down the bench (covered by a mat), finishing with your feet astride the bench. Take your weight on one foot and move straight into a cartwheel (or practise a backward roll across the mat into standing; twist into a cartwheel).	Grip the bench – work hard on the hands to clear the head of the bench. Stretch the legs to reach the floor. Work on good transition. Start low down on the bench.
2	Group 2 – Begin on the bench: carefully perform a round-off from the bench to the floor (or practise a cartwheel across the bench putting the first hand on the bench and the second on the floor).	*The teacher might need to remain at this station.* Check the position of the hands on the bench for this first task. For the alternative task the body will be moving quite quickly as the hand touches the floor.

3	Group 3 – Swing from a rope to land on the bench facing the rope. Let go. As the rope returns, jump on to it and swing back to your starting place (or practise swinging from a rope to land on the bench).	Children need to turn before landing. Ensure the rope is not snaking before jumping on to it.
4	Group 4 – From the floor, forward roll up the incline. Finish in a straddle either side of plank. Push off to one foot and move into a round-off (or practise round-offs on the floor).	A gentle push is needed to raise the hips and help the rotation up the plank. Stretch the legs after the push. Grip the plank with both hands to help you to finish in the straddle position.
5	Group 5 – Make a strong approach run, hurdle step from the floor to the springboard. Jump to land on the mat.	This happened naturally in an earlier stage from a bench. Think of a one-footed take-off from the floor into a two-footed take-off from the springboard.
6	Group 6 – Begin on the bench. Push carefully up into a headstand on a low bar box. Twist your feet to land on the mat (or practise headstands on a separate mat).	Push to initiate inversion then control the legs into the headstand. Work hard on the arms – grip the box.
7	Group 7 – Match a movement on the movement table and a movement on the floor.	Variety can be found by experimenting with leg shape.
8	Group 8 – Practise any combination of skills you have learned.	Watch for children simply repeating the same thing. Encourage them to watch others and try other combinations and to teach one another.
9	With a partner, choose your own apparatus (you may need to limit this depending on availability) and design the layout. Plan, practise and perform a sequence that combines some of the tasks in 1–7 above.	Verbalise responses. Select one or two examples to show. *This will take a long time for the children to perfect, so be prepared to use several lessons as appropriate.*
10	Provide opportunities for all children to show.	Encourage children to focus on individual pairs and feed back against whether actions have been combined with control and precision.

Final activity

As sessions 2 and 3.

Classroom

Children should make a note of their sequence with their partner to use later, and identify what they thought they did well and what they need to do to improve for the next lesson.

Revising previous actions – bridging, balancing, twisting, turning, springing, and symmetrical and asymmetrical body shapes with a partner and in groups

(A CD player, iPod station or similar will be needed for this session.)

Consolidation from previous session: to revise and further develop basic skills.

LEARNING OBJECTIVES

(The objectives of the session need to be made explicit to the children. They also need to assess the extent to which they have achieved them.)

Physical

1 To know a range of compositional principles to improve performance, for example level, direction and speed, working in unison and using mirroring, matching and working in canon.

2 To be able to combine a range of actions in a sequence with control and consistency.

Well-being

3 To know how to prepare the body for gymnastics.

Broader learning

4 To compose a sequence so that it reflects the beat of the music.

ASSESSMENT CRITERIA – QUESTIONS TO CONSIDER

1 Do the children include a range of compositional principles to improve performance, for example level, direction and speed, working in unison and canon, and using mirroring and matching?

2 Can they replicate a sequence of actions that they have planned, which demonstrates strong body control?

3 Are they able to perform activities that prepare the body for gymnastics?

4 Can they time their actions, working with the music?

Warm-up

	Content	Teaching points
1	Run in and out of each other (adding changes of direction, speed, levels and pathways) and on the sound of the tambour take your weight on your hands.	Encourage stretched limbs and strong tension throughout the body.
2	Run in and out of each other (adding changes of direction, speed, levels and pathways) and on the sound of the tambour travel into your action.	Verbalise responses. Expect control moving onto the hands.
3	Run in and out of each other (adding changes of direction, speed, levels and pathways) and on the sound of the tambour travel into and out of your action and select another way to travel around the hall.	As above.
	DEVELOPING SUPPLENESS AND STRENGTH – Encourage children, in pairs, to share ideas and actions that develop both suppleness and strength. Demonstrate good examples with the whole class who then try these themselves.	

Floor work

	Content	Teaching points
1	With a partner, plan a sequence that includes several of the following actions: balance, roll, jump, bridge and an action where you take your weight on your hands. Plan, practise and refine.	Task cards may help as a reminder. Balance: counterbalance and counter-tension (see Year 5, sessions 2 and 3 and sessions 4 and 5). Roll: teddy bear, log, forward, backward, sideways shoulder etc. (see 'Specific skills guide' – Rolling, page 227). Jump: star, scissor, tuck, pike etc.
2	Explore the order of your sequence. Consider ways of working together, for example starting together/apart, moving apart and then together, matching actions, moving at different levels, moving in the same or different directions, or varying the speed of your actions. Plan, practise and refine.	Encourage children to count to assist with timing. Select children to show, and highlight how variation in direction, speed and levels improves the look of the composition.
3	In pairs, show another pair your sequence. Then teach each other parts of your sequence.	You will need to organise the pairs carefully and give support.

	INTRODUCE MUSIC – encourage the children to listen to it carefully and think about how it might accompany their work. (See again 'The place of music', page 14.)	
4	Work together on a group sequence that includes some of the actions from each of the paired sequences. Explore the different ways of working together (as outlined above) and where you work in unison and canon or use mirroring or matching.	Encourage children to work in a variety of ways and select groups to show and highlight criteria. Allow time for groups to develop their sequences and circulate to give formative feedback.
5	Make sure your sequence has actions that are performed symmetrically, asymmetrically, and with twisting and turning (you may need to add to your sequence).	Verbalise and select one or two groups to show part or all of their sequence and highlight some of the criteria above. Discuss how they might use the beat of the music. Allow time for groups to develop their sequences and circulate to give formative feedback.
6	Groups are to perform to the whole class.	Focus children's attention on particular groups and encourage feedback against criteria used. Children should make a note of feedback to develop in the next session.

Final activity
As sessions 2 and 3.

Classroom
Children should make a note of their group sequence and the feedback to use later, and identify what they thought they did well and what they need to do to improve for the next lesson.

Revising previous actions and performing them on apparatus, and emphasising contrasts in speed, shape and levels

(A CD player, iPod station or similar will be needed for this session.)

Consolidation from previous session: to perform group sequences that include one or more of the following actions: balance, roll, jump, bridge and an action where weight is transferred to the hands.

LEARNING OBJECTIVES

(The objectives of the session need to be made explicit to the children. They also need to assess the extent to which they have achieved them.)

Physical

1   To know a range of compositional principles to improve performance using the apparatus, for example contrasting speed, shape and levels.

2   To be able to combine a range of actions in a sequence with control and consistency.

Well-being

3   To articulate how activity contributes to a healthy lifestyle.

Broader learning

4   To compose a sequence so that it reflects the beat of the music.

ASSESSMENT CRITERIA – QUESTIONS TO CONSIDER

1   Do the children show contrasting speed, shape and levels in their performance on the apparatus?

2   Can they replicate a sequence of actions that they have planned that demonstrates strong body control?

3   Can children describe some ways in which activity will support their lifestyle?

4   Can they time their actions, working with the music?

*Working on apparatus: (a) flight off,
(b) squat jumping on and (c) gripping
and balancing.*

(a)

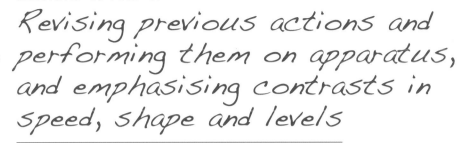

SESSIONS 16 AND 17

Revising previous actions and performing them on apparatus, and emphasising contrasts in speed, shape and levels

(A CD player, iPod station or similar will be needed for this session.)

Consolidation from previous session: to perform group sequences that include one or more of the following actions: balance, roll, jump, bridge and an action where weight is transferred to the hands.

LEARNING OBJECTIVES

(The objectives of the session need to be made explicit to the children. They also need to assess the extent to which they have achieved them.)

Physical

1   To know a range of compositional principles to improve performance using the apparatus, for example contrasting speed, shape and levels.

2   To be able to combine a range of actions in a sequence with control and consistency.

Well-being

3   To articulate how activity contributes to a healthy lifestyle.

Broader learning

4   To compose a sequence so that it reflects the beat of the music.

ASSESSMENT CRITERIA – QUESTIONS TO CONSIDER

1   Do the children show contrasting speed, shape and levels in their performance on the apparatus?

2   Can they replicate a sequence of actions that they have planned that demonstrates strong body control?

3   Can children describe some ways in which activity will support their lifestyle?

4   Can they time their actions, working with the music?

Warm-up

	Content	Teaching points
1	In groups of four, one child leads the others through a short warm-up routine.	Make sure that the intensity starts slowly and gradually increases. Try to include some of the actions learned previously.
2	Change over so that another child leads the warm-up. (*Make sure any child who has not led the warm-up has the opportunity to do so.*)	Can you think of different movements and actions? Why do we warm up?
3	Discuss as a whole class how being active contributes to a healthy lifestyle.	Expect responses relating to (a) physical development, including that of the muscles and heart, mobility of joints, strength, suppleness, speed, stamina etc.; (b) motor skill development: stability, locomotion etc.; (c) social development: negotiating, sharing ideas, working together etc.; and (d) cognitive development: planning ideas etc.
	DEVELOPING SUPPLENESS AND STRENGTH – Encourage children, in pairs, to share ideas and actions that develop both suppleness and strength. Demonstrate good examples with the whole class who then try these themselves.	

Floor work

	Content	Teaching points
1	In your groups, remind yourself of your sequence from the last session and practise it a couple of times through.	They should have recorded this and can use the notes made. Circulate and support.
2	Look at the feedback you received after your performance. Can you use this to develop your sequence further?	Circulate and support.
	INTRODUCE MUSIC again (see 'The place of music', page 14).	
3	Try to see if your actions can reflect the beat of the music.	Select one or two clear examples. It is important that the children are not hindered by the detailed flow of the music.

Apparatus

Children should choose their own apparatus and design the layout. *Make sure it is safe before they use it.*

	Content	Teaching points
1	Without music, adapt, practise and refine your sequence on to the apparatus and floor. Find actions that you can all do quickly.	There should be jumps, some rolls, runs, some inversions, recoil from twist and pivot. Encourage actions on, off, across apparatus etc.
2	Repeat, looking for slow actions.	Include balance, bridges, preparation into twist, rolls etc.
3	Practise working in your group where you contrast speed.	Remember you can cross each other, use each other, work towards, away etc. Select one or two groups to show.
4	Try now to modify some of these by also contrasting the shape. Try different actions where the body is generally tucked.	Expect weight on the hands with legs tucked, tucked jumps, rolls, balance etc.
5	Repeat with stretched actions.	Bending or curling may be necessary to *initiate* some actions.
6	Now experiment with changing your action and changing shape and speed.	For example, try quick tucked jumps into slow stretched balances. Stay with this for a while in order to find and share many possibilities.
7	Try to incorporate changes of level. Where you may be high on your apparatus or in your group, some may be high and others low. Explore and build into your sequence.	Allow time for the children to explore and share ideas.
8	Practise and refine your sequences and try to reflect the beat of the music in your performance.	Reintroduce the music here. Allow plenty of time for this.
9	Groups are to perform to the whole class.	Focus children on particular groups and encourage feedback against the criteria used. Make brief notes for later discussion.

Final activity

As previous session. Encourage children to bring their own music for the following session's composition.

Classroom

Children should make a more detailed note of their group sequence to use next time, and identify what they thought they did well and what they need to do to improve for the next lesson.

(a)

Working on apparatus: (a) flight off, (b) squat jumping on and (c) gripping and balancing.

YEAR 6: THE SESSIONS

(b)

(c)

Performance preparation

(A CD player, iPod station or similar will be needed for this session.)

Consolidation from previous session: to perform actions on the apparatus, emphasising contrasts in speed, shape and levels.

LEARNING OBJECTIVES

(The objectives of the session need to be made explicit to the children. They also need to assess the extent to which they have achieved them.)

Physical

1   To be able to devise a sequence responding to a given task.

2   To be able to combine a range of actions in a sequence with control and consistency.

Well-being

3   To articulate how activity contributes to a healthy lifestyle.

Broader learning

4   To assess each other's skills and abilities and plan a sequence accordingly.

ASSESSMENT CRITERIA – QUESTIONS TO CONSIDER

1   Do the children achieve up to eight to ten elements in their final performance?

2   Does their work demonstrate strong body control?

3   Can they describe some ways in which activity will support their lifestyle?

4   Are they able to adapt actions to cater for each other's ability?

Warm-up

	Content	Teaching points
1	In groups of four, one child is to lead others through a short warm-up routine.	Make sure that the intensity starts slowly and gradually increases. Try to include some of the previous actions learned.
2	Change over so that another child leads the warm-up.	Can you think of different movements and actions? Why do we warm up?
3	Discuss as a whole class how being active contributes to a healthy lifestyle.	Expect responses relating to (a) physical development, including that of the muscles and heart, mobility of joints, strength, suppleness, speed, stamina etc.; (b) motor skill development: stability, locomotion etc.; (c) social development: negotiating, sharing ideas, working together etc.; and (d) cognitive development: planning ideas etc.

> **DEVELOPING SUPPLENESS AND STRENGTH** – Encourage children, in pairs, to share ideas and actions that develop both suppleness and strength. Demonstrate good examples with the whole class who then try these themselves.

Floor work

Over the next two sessions children will be set a task that they will then perform as part of the assessment task in the final session.

	Content	Teaching points
1	In groups of three or four compose a sequence that includes up to eight to ten elements.	Task cards may act as a reminder or write on the board. They should include twisting and turning, counterbalance and counter-tension, symmetrical and asymmetrical shapes, and contact with obstacles.
2	Plan, practise and refine. Remind children of composition principles: changes in level, direction and speed.	Select one or two to show.
3	Plan, practise and refine.	Remind children of different ways of working together: mirroring, matching, in unison and canon, and encourage pairs within groups to contrast (if working in fours).
4	Plan, practise, refine.	Differentiate tasks for each group depending on ability (make the sequences longer/shorter), for example include more ways of travelling, body shapes, balance, rolls, jumps etc.
5	Consider how you move towards and away, start at different times etc. in your sequence. Play around with the order of your actions to make the sequence more interesting and pleasing to an audience.	Children may need to initially count out loud to perfect timing. Circulate and give formative feedback. Record groups and play back so they can self-evaluate (work with a teaching assistant on this).
6	In your group, decide on the piece of music you want to use (one of your own or one from the school). Adapt your sequence to the music.	Have *short* compilations available. *Check the language suitability of music brought from home!* The groups may have to take turns with using the music. Circulate and support.
7	Groups are to show their sequence to another group.	Peer-assess and feed back on something that each group can work on.
8	Work on feedback to develop your sequence.	Circulate and support.

Apparatus

Children should choose their own apparatus and design the layout. *Make sure it is safe before they use it.*

	Content	Teaching points
1	Adapt your sequence to include apparatus. Practise and refine your sequence on to apparatus and floor (use the selected music).	Circulate and support. The groups may have to take turns with using the music.
2	Consider how you move towards and away, start at different times etc. in your sequence and play around with the order of your actions to make it more interesting and pleasing to an audience. Think about the timing of actions to music.	Children may need to initially count out loud to perfect timing. Circulate and give formative feedback. With a teaching assistant, record groups and play back so they can self-evaluate.
3	Groups are to show their sequence to another group.	Peer-assess and feed back on something that each group can work on.
4	Work on feedback to develop your sequence.	Circulate and support.
5	Continue to practise in preparation for the final assessment performance or performing to an audience.	Circulate and support. Children are to record the sequence, apparatus design and music title.

Final activity

As previous session.

Classroom

Children should finalise the notes of their performances, and identify what they thought they did well and what they still might need to do to improve for the final performance.

Assessment activity

(A CD player, iPod station or similar will be needed for this session.)

This session will assess children's knowledge and understanding gained from the sessions throughout the year. Children should be encouraged to take responsibility for their own learning by identifying what they can achieve, what they need to do to develop and how they will do this.

LEARNING OBJECTIVES

(The objectives of the session need to be made explicit to the children. They also need to assess the extent to which they have achieved them.)

Physical

1   To perform a sequence of contrasting actions in groups.

2   To adapt the sequence performed on the floor to include both the floor and apparatus.

3   To remember and perform the sequence with consistency, coordination and control.

Well-being

4   To know that strength and suppleness are key attributes of a gymnast.

Broader learning

5   To compose their sequence so it reflects the beat of the music.

DISCUSSION

Discuss and share ideas of the key attributes of a gymnast and why being strong and supple is important.

Talk about what constitutes good work and how improvements can be made.

ASSESSMENT CRITERIA – QUESTIONS TO CONSIDER

1   Can the children, in groups, perform contrasting actions in a sequence?

2   Can they adapt their sequence from the floor to include both the floor and apparatus?

3   Can they remember and perform the sequence with consistency, coordination and control?

4   Can the children talk about what a gymnast needs to develop physically and so improve their performance?

5   Can they time their actions, working with the music?

OUTCOME

Some children will achieve, some will excel and some will achieve less.

Warm-up

Children will take turns in their group of four in leading the warm-up in preparation for their final performance. This should include stretching.

Apparatus

	Content	Teaching points
1	In your group, rehearse your sequence (from the previous session) with music, in preparation for your final performance. Perform the finished sequence.	This can take place with an audience or in front of the whole class. The teacher will assess sequences (in conjunction with a teaching assistant where applicable) against the above criteria. These should also be recorded and a copy made available for the children's Key Stage 3 school.

Final activity

The teacher leads a final stretching warm-down with the whole class.

Classroom

Celebrate the work achieved.

Specific skills guide

1 Running

Running is an activity that is seldom taught and that is used mainly for warm-up purposes. Few children, as a result, run well, that is, in a mechanically efficient manner. Some of the faults that one can observe in children's running are pointed out below with appropriate corrective action. The teacher should use the corrective action as positive teaching points and encourage children to work on these aspects.

Fault	Correct action
Running with flat feet, producing a slapping action on the floor.	Run on the 'balls' of the feet (check the child doesn't have dropped arches). Encourage ankle extension.
Running with the feet or knees turned outwards or inwards.	Run concentrating on the feet pointing ahead. Run along a line.
Running with straight legs.	Bend at the knees and emphasise knee lift.
Running with straight arms.	Bend arms to 90° at the elbows and punch with the arms. Illustrate the effect of the arms by asking children to jog on the spot and then speed up the arms only. In 99 cases out of a 100, the legs will automatically increase in speed.

| Running in too upright a position. | Demonstrate that little ground is covered in this way. A lean forward is necessary to produce a longer stride. This should be demonstrated to the children. |
| Not running in a straight line and/or with the head turning from side to side. | Run along a line on the floor and fix the eyes on a spot ahead. |

Any child who appears to have a serious problem with flat feet should be referred to his/her doctor for remedial treatment.

2 Jumping/landing

The most important aspect of jumping, paradoxically, is landing. The children should be taught to land on the balls of the feet with immediate lowering of the heels and a slight bend of the knees to end up in a stable position (Figure 1). (Saying 'toe–heel' helps this feeling.)

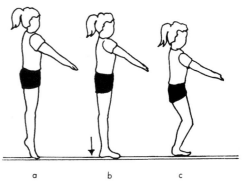

Figure 1.

This should be done initially on mats to avoid jarring. The bottom should be above the heels and the back should be relatively straight (1c). The children should be asked to squat low and observe what happens to their heels. (The heels lift up, thus creating a small base of support and, therefore, a less stable landing position.) Jumping practices should be on the spot at first, then with a couple of steps and, finally, after a short run. Children should try to get their feet slightly ahead of their bodies to establish a secure landing, otherwise forward momentum will cause them to overbalance forward. Later, jumps from a low height can be introduced.

Take-off and airborne phase (including hurdle step)

Normally, take-off is from two feet and children can experience difficulty in coordinating the step before this moment of take-off (the hurdle step).

The take off can be performed from the floor or from a springboard (or Reuther board).

A useful preliminary stage is as follows:

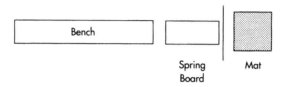

The child walks from halfway along the bench, drops naturally on to two feet on the springboard and jumps up and on to the mat. (Thus the one foot to two feet pattern is established.)

Develop this by a gentle run, rather than a walk.

Then: the full and correct hurdle step (take-off) action is as shown in Figure 2.

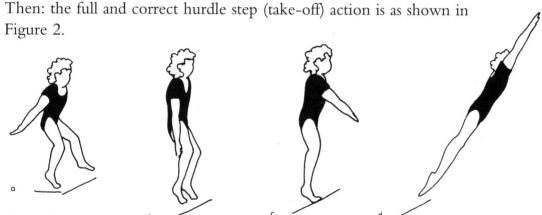

Figure 2.

(a) Arms back. Long, low jump from one foot. Arms begin to swing forward strongly.

(b) Arms come through on approach to springboard (or take-off point).

(c) Arms still lifting.

(d) Arms assist full stretch. Legs and ankles fully extended. (Note position of arms in relation to head.)

Jumps with quarter, half and full turns

All turning and twisting movements of this nature start while the feet are in contact with the ground. The important point for the children to understand is that, as the arms lift up in the jump, the head and shoulders turn slightly in the intended direction without any dropping of the shoulders (Figure 3). The arms must remain fairly close together if the turn is to occur easily. To stop rotation, the arms drop from above the head to shoulder height. Body tension should be retained throughout. A lack of tension, especially in the stomach region, will tend to cause unstable landing positions.

Figure 3.

3 Forward roll

This should be done on mats and not on the floor.

A good general principle when teaching gymnastics skills is to start with the last part and work back to the beginning. This is not always possible, but by using this method the pupil can always finish a movement, and is not moving into the 'unknown', which causes stress and fear.

The finished roll should look like the drawings in Figure 4.

It is important that:

1   hands are flat;

2   the action goes *forward*;

3   from 4b a good push is made to ensure straight legs into the piked position as in 4c;

4   feet then tuck in really close to the bottom;

5   arms reach *forward and up* to stand.

The teaching stages are:

1   Rock backwards and forwards (Figure 5) emphasising heels close to the bottom and chin to the chest. If the feet are away from the

bottom at point (d) in Figure 4, they exert a force backwards that prevents the child standing up.

2 The arms should reach forward in Figure 5c; a partner's hands can be caught or grasped to encourage this action.

3 The child stands feet astride, hands on the floor near the feet but shoulder width apart. He/she then tucks chin to chest and lowers the top of the shoulders to the floor and tips over to roll. The moment the rolls starts, the child carries out the actions shown in Figure 4c–e.

4 The child attempts the roll from a squat position (Figure 4b–d).

Figure 5.

Figure 4.

Variation of forward roll – forward roll to straddle stand

This roll involves flexibility in the hips – the wider the legs the easier the move.

Figure 6.

As the roll comes towards the ground, the legs part (Figure 6). Before the legs come to the ground (b), the hands reach to the ground between the legs – shoulders should be well in front of hips – and then the hands push to bring the body up on the feet.

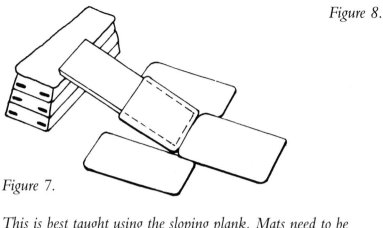

Figure 7.

Figure 8.

a

b

This is best taught using the sloping plank. Mats need to be placed on the planks alongside and at the bottom of the plank (Figure 7). The pupil's feet are placed either side of the plank when finishing the roll, which makes the whole move much easier and, above all, successful (Figure 8).

Slowly lower the planks and eventually dispense with them altogether.

4 Backward roll

The backward roll should look like the drawings in Figure 9.

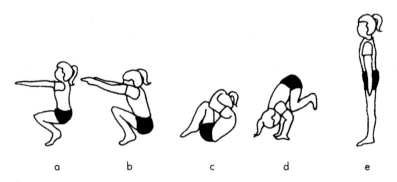

a   b   c   d   e

Figure 9.

It is important that:

1   hands are held in position early;

2   hands are placed flat on the floor close to the head (fingers pointing towards feet, thumbs to head);

3   knees and head are tucked tightly to the chest;

4   when the hips move over the head, the child pushes hard from the hands and stays tucked;

5   the child keeps pushing and lands on the *feet* (not the knees).

The teaching stages are as follows:

1   Rock backwards and forwards emphasising heels close to the bottom and chin to the chest.

Ask children what would get in the way to stop them going right over backwards? *Answer: The head.*

How can we get the head out of the way? *By lifting the body over it by using the arms* (Figure 9d).

2   Now rock backwards and ensure that the push comes when the knees and hips are above the hands so that it lifts and does not thrust the child back from where he/she has come.

3   Finally, the whole roll can be done from squat and stand (Figure 9).

4   A variation of the backward roll is to a straddle stand.

5 Headstand

The basis of a good headstand is a good base of support (Figure 10).

Figure 10 Plan view of the base of support.

The teaching stages are:

1   Place the hands and head on the mat as shown in a kneeling position (Figure 11a). Straighten the legs (11b) so that the weight is on the hands and head. Then walk carefully towards the nose until the bottom is over the head (11c).

Figure 11a–e.

2 Now bend the legs up so that the feet are by the bottom (Figure 11d).

3 When this can be achieved confidently, the legs can be straightened (Figure 11e).

In order to roll out of the headstand, tell the children to put '*chin to chest*' and gently roll out.

6 Handstand

The handstand requires strong arms and shoulder girdle and the ability of the child to hold the body tense. Without this basic body tension, 'banana'-type handstands with their attendant undesirable physical effects will occur. The handstand is an inverted standing position. A plumb line dropped from the ankles should pass through the knee, hip, shoulder and wrist (Figure 12a).

Figure 12.

SPECIFIC SKILLS GUIDE

The teaching stages are as follows:

Preparatory stage:

1 The child should lie down on the back, arms above the head. He/she tenses the body. This is the feeling to be achieved when on the hands, and also the body shape required, that is, a straight line.

2 The child now kneels on the floor, hands flat and pointing forward in front of the knees. The child then straightens the legs (Figure 13).

a   b

Figure 13.

Safety: Emphasise flat hands, fingers pointing forward and shoulder width apart. Head should be looking *just in front of the fingers*.

3 Repeat (2). When the legs are straight, swing one up into the air straight, pushing gently with the other leg and feeling the tendency for it to lift off the ground.

4 Repeat, but this time exchange legs in the air – that is, as the first leg starts to come back to the ground the second legs swings up.

5 The child stands arms above head and steps forward as for a handstand, and swings one leg up into the air straight, with sufficient speed to lift the other leg just off the ground.

6 Handstand with teacher support (Figures 14 and 15).

Figure 14 Initial support position.
NB: Supporter's head by child's hip to avoid being kicked in the face.

Figure 15 Support when child is able to perform a handstand.

7   The finished action should look like the drawings in Figure 16.

Figure 16.

It is important that:

1   hands are flat and shoulder width apart; fingers are forward, with arms straight;

(ii) eyes look at the hands;

(iii) the movement is 'step forward – reach forward' – gently (the step forward action is the lunge step);

(iv) hips are above the shoulders and the body is straight.

Safety: in the case of overbalancing – step one of the hands forward. The feet will then come down sideways.

7 Cartwheel

The cartwheel, as the name implies, is a wheeling action involving rotation on the four points of the body – hand, hand, foot, foot – each contacting the ground successively in an even rhythm.

The finished action should look like the drawings in Figure 17.

Figure 17.

The following sequence is important:

1   Begin forwards, step strongly forwards with the foot pointing *in the direction* of the action.

2   The chest goes down to the knee of the bent leg.

3   Hands are at right angles to the line of action.

Figure 17a.

4   Push hard from the bent leg and swing the other up – straddle the legs wide.

5   Arms should be straight.

6   Eyes should be looking downwards.

Figure 18.

The teaching stages are:

1   The child stands at one end of a bench with his/her left side towards it, as in Figure 18. The child steps forward on to this left foot, placing the left hand on the bench followed by the right hand. As the right foot comes to the floor, followed by the left, the child will turn to end up with the back to the bench.

2   The child tries to get the foot higher in performing the cartwheel. The teacher will have to support many children at this stage.

3   The whole should now be attempted on mats, or along a straight line on the floor.

8 Round-off

The finished action should look like the drawings in Figure 19.

Figure 19.

The round-off differs from the cartwheel as follows:

1   It is generally performed with more speed and often finishes with a jump from two feet.

2   There are two quarter turns of the body and the direction therefore changes from initial forward movement to final backward position.

3   It would normally begin with a hurdle step (see 'Jumping', page 217).

Note: the hand placings are crucial to successful turning within the action. The legs snap together at the top of the action.

The teaching stages can be:

1   cartwheel;

2   handstand/snap down;

3   lunge step to round-off (that is, not hurdle step approach);

4   standing hurdle step to round off;

5   one or two steps into hurdle step to round off.

9 Simple variations in rolling

Log roll

Feet together, toes and fingers fully extended, and weight taken on the hips.

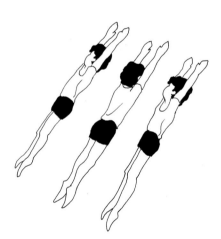

Roll with one leg leading

As for the log roll but the high leg moves across the body to start the movement.

Teddy bear roll

Straddle sit with leg extension and body tension. Take hold of the lower legs or ankles. Lower the body to the side so that the shoulder or side of the body is on the floor. Roll across the back and sit up facing the opposite direction. Keep the legs in the astride position throughout the roll.

Sideways shoulder roll

Highlight the starting position. Drop the leading shoulder to start the movement, roll across the shoulders keeping the knees bent. Keep the momentum going and roll over to replicate the starting position.

Tuck and stretch roll

Tuck and stretch alternately.

Apparatus diagrams and task cards

The following diagrams of apparatus patterns are proposed for specific sessions:

Year 4: sessions 4 and 5

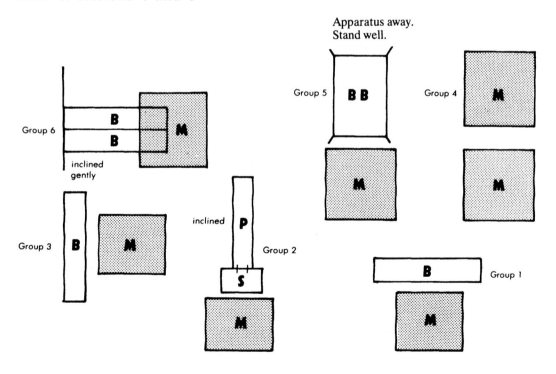

Year 5: sessions 10 and 11

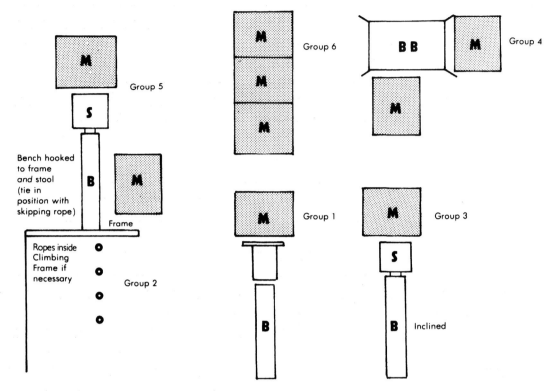

Note: Group 2 & 5 Use ropes & wall frame separately.

Year 6: sessions 12 and 13

For details of this session see under 'Session plan task cards' (page 232).

Using task cards

Preparing task cards for particular sessions enables the teacher to set differentiated tasks for different groups of children. Also, they enable the children to read and assimilate the task themselves.

It is sometimes useful to give children task cards that incorporate a drawing of the task required. The examples below of ideas for counterbalance and counter-tension will provide a focus for trying out the movements.

Task cards do not take very long to prepare. Teachers could copy the ideas listed below on to cards quite easily.

APPARATUS DIAGRAMS AND TASK CARDS

Session plan task cards

Year 4, sessions 4 and 5

Group 1

Find ways to combine rolls and jumps using the floor and the apparatus. Make sure you include a turn when you jump.

Group 2

Travel up the plank, gripping it with your hands, jumping your feet from one side to the other. Explore a range of jumps and rolls when you dismount.

Group 3

Take a short approach run to the bench, take off from one foot to land on two feet on the bench. Jump off to land on the mat. Vary the shape of the jump in the air.

Group 4

Practise forward and backward rolls, trying to vary the shape of the legs during the roll.

Group 5

Squat jump on to the box. Spring off showing a clear stretched body shape in the air before landing.

Group 6

Practise a straddle forward roll carefully down the slope.

Year 5, sessions 10 and 11

Group 1

1 Walk along the bench, hurdle step to the springboard, spring off to land on the mat.
2 Slowly run along the bench, hurdle step to the springboard. Immediately take off and vary shape of your jump on to the mat.

Group 2

1 Take two steps, jump to swing on to the rope to land on the mat.
2 Take two steps, spring and grip the rope, release and land on the mat facing the place you started from.

Group 3

1 Begin on the bench, take your weight on your hands and push off to the floor. Roll away from the landing.
2 Walk to near the top of the bench. Take your weight on to your hands on the stool and push off, to take your feet round the stool to land on the mat.

Group 4

1 Squat jump from the floor to the box – step and spring off on to the mat.
2 Squat jump on to the box. Lie on the box. Place a hand carefully on the mat and do a forward roll.

Group 5

1 Practise swinging your legs from one side of bench to the other by taking your weight on your hands. Develop this by gaining flight in the second phase from your hands.

2 From the floor, squat jump on to the stool. Jump off showing a clear body shape.

Group 6

1 Revise the round-off. From a short approach run, skip, step into the round off and take this into a springing action.

Year 6, sessions 12 and 13

Select 5 or 6 of these to suit your situation.

Group 1: bench inclined to low rung of stool; mat and one extra mat

Backward roll down the bench (covered by a mat) finishing with your feet astride the bench. Take your weight on one foot and move straight into a cartwheel (or practise backward roll across the mat into standing. Twist into a cartwheel).

Group 2: benches

Begin on the bench: carefully perform a round-off from the bench to the floor (or practise a cartwheel across the bench, putting the first hand on the bench and the second on the floor).

Group 3: ropes and bench

Swing from the rope to land on the bench facing the ropes. Let go. As the rope returns to you, jump on to it and swing back to your starting place (or practise swinging from the rope to land on the bench).

Group 4: plank inclined to low rung of climbing frame; mat on plank

Starting on the floor, forward roll up the incline. Finish in straddle either side of plank. Push off to one foot and move into a round-off (or practise round-offs on the floor).

Group 5: springboard and mat

Strong approach run, hurdle step from the floor to the springboard. Jump off to land on the mat.

Group 6: bench: low bar box, mat and extra mat

Begin on the bench. Push carefully up to a headstand on a low bar box. Twist your feet to land on the mat (or practise headstands on the separate mat).

Group 7: movement table and mats

Match a movement on the movement table and a movement on the floor.

Group 8: a run of mats

Practise any combination of skills that you have learned.

Ideas for counterbalance and counter-tension (see Year 5, sessions 2 and 3 and sessions 4 and 5).